Integrating health
and social care
and making it work

Margaret Edwards and Clive Miller

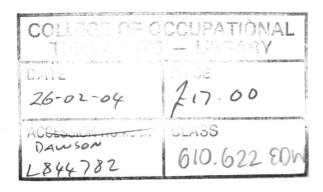

© June 2003, OPM™
252B Gray's Inn Road
London WC1X 8XG
tel: 020 7239 7800
fax: 020 7837 5800

email: office@opm.co.uk
website: www.opm.co.uk

A companion OPM publication, *Integrating Children's Services: Issues and Practice*, which investigates the cross-sector integration of services for children and their families, is also available.

OPM is a registered trademark of the Office for Public Management Limited.

Editing and design: Leila Carlyle

Printed by The Hackney Press

ISBN: 1 898531 79 X

Contents

Acronyms used in this book

We have used many acronyms in this book. They are listed below. A number in brackets after an acronym points to the page where it is first used or defined.

CPA   Care Programme Approach [17]
CPPIH   Commission for Patient and Public Involvement in Health [30]
DoH   Department of Health
DPA   Data Protection Act; *also* Data Protection Agency [72]
e-government   electronic government [62]
GP   general practitioner
HA   health authority
HAZ   health action zone [6]
HIMP   health improvement plan [69]
HRA   Housing Revenue Account [40]; also Human Rights Act [72]
ICAS   Independent Complaints Advocacy Services [30]
ICT   information and communication technology [61]
IeG   Implementing e-Government [statement] [64]
LA   local authority
LIP   local implementation plan [69]
LIS   local implementation strategy [69]
LSP   local strategic partnership [6]
NELH   National Electronic Library for Health [62]
NHS   National Health Service
NICE   National Institute for Clinical Excellence [43]
NPSA   the National Patient Safety Agency [30]
PALS   Patient Advisory and Liaison Service [30]
PCT   primary care trust [4]
SCIE   Social Care Institute for Excellence [59]
SHA   strategic health authority [4]
SLA   service level agreement [2]
SSD   social services department [1]
TOPSS   Training Organisation for the Personal Social Services [53]-

Preface

This publication examines the practical implications of achieving greater integration between health and social care services. It concentrates mostly on services for adults. A companion OPM publication *Integrating Children's Services: Issues and Practice*, by Clive Miller and Ann McNicholl, investigates the cross-sector integration of services for children and their families.

We have drawn extensively on OPM's wider experience of health and social care integration, especially on the insights gained from a series of senior management learning networks we have organised on health and social care integration. Participants on these networks set their own agendas and worked on the 'live' issues they were experiencing, and their agendas have helped us structure this publication. Apart from focusing on integration, the networks also explored the nuts and bolts of how health and social care organisations carry out core tasks such as commissioning and financial management. We have built on this by providing brief descriptions of current health and social care systems, practices and national drivers of change.

Our thanks go to our colleagues: Ruth Davis for much background research; and Jude Cummins at OPM, David Hunter at the Foundation for Information Technology in Local Government, and Adrienne Fresko at OPM for help with the chapters on involving people, information & ICT and governance, respectively.

While we acknowledge the help of learning network members and the invaluable contribution of the OPM editorial team, responsibility for the final publication lies firmly with the authors.

Margaret Edwards and Clive Miller
April 2003

Chapter one: The policy context

A significant number of people in the UK require a combination of support from public services to help them to live as independently as possible. As more people live longer or have long-term health needs, the number of people requiring this support grows. Their needs, however, have not always been met. We know that one important reason why is that the responsibility for commissioning[1] or providing care has been divided up between different organisations, with no common mechanisms for co-ordination, either at the strategic level or at the individual level.

The NHS and Community Care Act, 1990 was an attempt to respond to this lack of co-ordination between health and social care. The Act introduced the concept of the 'care manager' who would be responsible for ensuring that all the health and social needs of an individual were assessed and their subsequent care co-ordinated. Care managers were to be employed by social services departments (SSDs) and, in practice, the majority of people appointed to these posts were qualified social workers.

The Act focused on responding to people with complex health and social care needs and giving them priority when resources were being allocated. It also introduced a requirement that the local authority (LA) – in consultation with colleagues in the National Health Service (NHS) and the voluntary sector and with service users themselves – must produce an annual 'community care plan' which set out its plans to improve services.

Subsequent government reports and other studies highlighted the continuing lack of co-ordination between health and social care, as well as the absence from local plans of other services like education and housing. Community care plans tended to be seen as being mainly the preserve of SSDs, with limited involvement from other services. Problems in co-ordinating care also arose because of barriers that tended to isolate professional groups within organisations, something the Act paid less attention to. One of the reasons that care managers were unable to co-ordinate care effectively was that they were genuinely unable to develop joint ways of working with other professionals, particularly with colleagues in health services. At the same time, limited progress was being made on developing joint assessment forms and working methods.

The Community Care Act encouraged social services to develop their role as purchasers of care. It provided LAs with funds to take on responsibility for people previously funded through Income Support, but 75 per cent of this money had to be spent on buying services from the independent sector. The Act also encouraged LAs to separate the functions of care management from those of service provision and develop service level agreements (SLAs) with their own ('in-house') providers. This was usually described as the 'purchaser/provider separation'. The stated aim of these two policy changes was to encourage LAs to negotiate with providers to obtain more responsive services.

Statutory social care continued to constitute a small proportion of the care provided to people with day-to-day needs. Informal care by family and friends was the largest source of support, and continues to be so.

Policy changes

A number of policy changes have taken place in England since the Community Care Act:

- The central role of LAs in promoting the health of their community has increasingly been recognised (see the Health Act, 1999 and the Health and Social Care Act, 2000). For example, the correlation between limited education, poverty and ill-health is acknowledged in policy documents and reflected in regeneration projects. LAs are expected to take a corporate approach to improving health by considering how services like leisure, housing, environmental services and town planning can contribute. The *Supporting People* policy that aims to co-ordinate support to individuals who need help to live independently at home is an example of this.
- The Community Care Act encouraged the concentration of resources on service users with the greatest and most complex needs. But the weakness of this approach became clear because pressures on health and social care kept increasing as, for example, the proportion of older people being admitted to hospital through accident and emergency departments continued to rise. So now people have started to focus their attention on preventing deterioration in health. For example, it is recognised that preventing falls in older people is an important way of avoiding long-term ill-health and social problems.
- The guidance on individual needs assessment in the Act took the position that users should be involved in the process, and the subsequent policy on carers introduced carers' assessments. Policy since then has emphasised this stance even more. National service frameworks, for instance, have emphasised that individuals can be experts in managing their own care, provided they are given enough information.
- The National Service Framework for Older People introduced a requirement for a single assessment process to cover the needs of individuals. Similar ways of working exist or are being developed in mental health and learning disability services.

- The success of the Independent Living Fund in enabling people to purchase cost-effective support encouraged a debate about the extension of these principles. LAs were given the power to offer 'direct payments' to people who had been assessed as needing support (Community Care [Direct Payments] Act, 1996), allowing them to purchase services directly rather than having them arranged through a care manager. At first, these powers were limited to certain adult groups, but they have now been extended to anyone over the age of 65 and people with learning disabilities.

When the reasons for the lack of co-ordination between health and local government were examined, it appeared that some barriers were cultural and some related to legal constraints. The most significant legal constraints were: the need for each organisation to be accountable for the money spent through an audit trail matching expenditure to volumes of work or individuals supported; and the grey area surrounding the potential for an organisation to devolve its responsibilities to another organisation.

In response to lobbying from the health and social care sectors to remove these constraints, the government started to develop new policies that resulted in the introduction of the Health Act, 1999.

The Health Act, 1999

In September 1998, the government published a consultation document called *Partnership in Action,* which contained ideas for improving joint working between health and social services. The intention was to remove barriers in the existing system that prevented vulnerable people from receiving integrated, needs-led services. By the time the proposals were converted into legislation in the Health Act, 1999, they included all the health-related functions of local government, and not just social services.

The Health Act introduced powers (from April 2000) to enable local government and the NHS to create new forms of partnership. The Act allows these powers to be used; it does not make them mandatory. However the *NHS Plan* (published after the Act) indicated that the government *would* in future require these powers to be used. The *NHS Plan* also introduced the concept of 'care trusts', which take the model of partnership further than the Act does, and which we will look at shortly.

Health Act 'flexibilities'

There are three types of arrangements, described in Section 31 of the Act as Health Act 'flexibilities':

- lead commissioning
- pooled budgets or funds
- integrated provision.

A quick look at the main features of each of these will be helpful at this point.

Lead commissioning

- One organisation – which could be a health authority (HA), primary care trust (PCT) or LA – takes on commissioning for a particular service on behalf of other organisations. With the creation of strategic health authorities (SHAs), the PCT or LA is most likely to be the lead organisation.
- Liability or accountability stays with the organisation that delegates responsibility for commissioning, typically the LA and one or more PCTs.
- Funds to purchase services are delegated to the lead commissioner. These must be spent in such a way as to reflect the financial contribution each organisation has made to the commissioning budget: i.e. NHS funds must be spent on NHS functions, and LA funds on LA functions.
- Services can be commissioned from any provider – public, private or voluntary.

Pooled budgets or funds

- Organisations (PCTs and LAs) pool their funds to meet specific objectives. Each agrees a level of contribution and the length of time the arrangement will operate (including periods of review, extensions and termination).
- Clear aims and objectives must be agreed at the beginning. The partner organisations will measure the value of their investment against these.
- The fund is meant to cover mainly revenue expenditure. Major capital costs need to be met through Sections 29 or 30 of the Act.
- One organisation 'hosts' the fund and appoints a single manager, who is responsible for overall spending and for reporting to the contributing partners on outputs and outcomes. The host organisation can sub-contract the management of funds to another, outside organisation.
- The host organisation identifies staff who will assess people's needs and purchase appropriate care using money from the pooled funds.
- Once in the pool, the funds can be used for any specified services that fall within the functions of the contributing organisations. Funds originating in the NHS can be used on LA functions and vice versa. (For example, LA staff can purchase health services).
- Funds can be used to purchase services from independent providers.
- Contributing organisations retain responsibility for their own work throughout the arrangement and will need to know to what extent the services that are being paid for via the pooled budget are fulfilling their own organisational objectives.

Integrated provision

- Particular services, previously provided by different organisations, are integrated by being brought together under a single management structure. These can include the assessment of individual needs and care planning.

- The role of 'integrated provider' (managing the service) can be taken on by an NHS or primary care trust or an LA.
- The integrated provider may provide all the services directly or, where appropriate, sub-contract with other independent providers for some of the service.
- The organisations that have transferred their responsibility to the integrated provider must monitor the effectiveness of the arrangements.
- All staff are managed by the integrated provider and can either be seconded from other organisations or directly employed.

Sections 29 and 30 of the Act

These two sections of the Act legislate for a way to transfer funds between organisations, providing alternatives to the flexibilities. The transfers will be contributions to specific services that the authority receiving the funds agrees to provide. The body transferring funds needs to be satisfied that the payment is likely to be a more effective use of public money than spending the equivalent amount on its own services. Funds can be used for revenue expenditure, but they can also cover large capital items that both organisations see as being essential to a service: in this way, one organisation will remain the clear owner of the building or equipment. A good example of this would be the transfer of funds to contribute to the purchase or lease of premises for an integrated one-stop service.

Section 29

Section 29 builds on previous legislation (Health Act, 1977) which allowed HAs to transfer funds to LAs and voluntary organisations for certain purposes. In the past, this was mainly to fund people with learning disabilities or mental health problems who were coming out of long-stay hospital and being cared for in the community. Section 29 extends these powers to cover all health-related functions of LAs and voluntary organisations and also gives these powers to PCTs.

Section 30

In the past, it was not possible for LAs to transfer funds to the NHS. Section 30 allows for this, and LAs can now transfer funds to PCTs and HAs for certain purposes, although not others. For example, surgical treatments and emergency ambulance services are excluded.

Care trusts

Having introduced the Health Act, the government expected to see the 'flexibilities' described within it taken up more quickly than they were. When progress on this was slow, the government then reinforced its expectations: it used the *NHS Plan* to require the use of flexibilities for some services in each locality and to introduce a new type of organisation, the 'care trust'. A care trust is a single, multi-purpose, legal body, set up to commission and provide local health and social care. Care trusts provide an alternative approach to integrating services: they are organisations based on either PCTs or NHS trusts, expanded to incorporate social care; therefore they are likely to be applied to larger areas of service. Perhaps for this reason, many LAs have viewed care trusts with suspicion. To date, the development of these new trusts has proceeded slowly, and it is still too early to evaluate their impact on outcomes for service users.

All in all, flexibilities and care trusts are being taken up, but slowly, mainly because introducing these models requires both the investment of management time and the accumulation of political will and trust. The ultimate test of the policy will be the extent to which adopting these new models leads to more integrated experiences for users and carers.

Other forms of strategic partnership

Over the last decade, several new government policies have highlighted the role of LAs in promoting economic regeneration and community development. The majority of these have assumed that LAs will take a central, co-ordinating role in developing partnerships with other organisations operating in their locality. Examples include:

- local strategic partnerships (LSPs), which bring together statutory, voluntary and private organisations to develop and implement plans for regeneration. LSPs oversee neighbourhood renewal plans, as well as the allocation of development monies.
- health action zones (HAZs), which are partnerships in local areas to promote health. These have varied in their membership but usually involve local government and health organisations playing major roles.
- scrutiny. The importance of the LA's role in promoting the health of its local community is underlined by the responsibility it now has for scrutinising local health services. This is another opportunity for partnership working; the scrutiny activity can feed into joint strategic planning.
- 'health partnership boards', which many localities now have, and which undertake planning work related to health and social care.

Devolution

While the policies in Scotland, Wales and Northern Ireland are distinct from those in England, they contain the same push towards increased integration of health and local government services.

Scotland

In Scotland, *Joint Futures*[1] is a policy intended to develop the joint funding and management of community care services through partnership structures, starting with services for older people. It includes joint assessment, the introduction of pooled budgets and shared information systems.

---

1. *Community Care: A Joint Future*, Scottish Executive, 2000

Wales

The Welsh Assembly created a Health and Well-being Partnership Council whose membership included health, local government and voluntary sector organisations along with service users.

'Local health groups' in Wales provide a focus for partnership work between health and local government: their work commissioning services is helped by the fact that health and local government authorities share the same geographical boundaries.

Northern Ireland

In Northern Ireland there are four 'health and social services boards' that plan, commission and monitor health and social services in their area. There are also nineteen 'health and social services trusts' that provide services for local populations.

Chapter two: Service integration

The term 'integration' is used to describe a variety of approaches to co-ordinating activities between organisations. Throughout this publication we are going to look at integration at three levels. We believe that looking at integration in this way will make it easier for you to analyse your organisation's activities and to clarify exactly where you will need to focus your efforts to increase and improve integration.

The three levels are:

individual service users and carers – activity that involves communicating with individuals and organising information and services for them.

service networks – the co-ordination and management of activities between care management, community nursing and primary care teams and between those teams and statutory, voluntary and private sector service providers. This is usually focused on a locality or a specialist service network.

the whole system – activities such as strategic planning, commissioning and managing the market of services for the whole population or service user groups in an area. This may be a PCT or LA area, or a geographically wider area such as the community care provider market or the wider 'health economy'.

Before we start examining integration on these three levels, we should look briefly at how a lack of integration can cause problems for service users and their carers who are trying to navigate what can be an extremely complex web of services.

How poorly co-ordinated services affect users and carers

Users and carers often find that, to have their needs properly met, they have to co-ordinate around themselves a set of services provided by different agencies. Their efforts to do so often fail because they lack the necessary knowledge about how the systems work, they are powerless to influence the decisions of individual workers and/or they do not have the time or energy to be their own care manager. Furthermore, as we described in chapter one, the creation of care manager posts in social services has not brought about either co-ordinated assessment of health and social needs or co-ordinated services.

The main problems are:

- **duplication of activities**. People with complex needs may find they are having their situation assessed several times, with each assessor asking for much the same information as before. This is time consuming for everyone, and is likely to prolong the whole process.
- **contradictory decisions**. Following assessment, separate decisions may be reached about the services a person needs. If there are no opportunities for dialogue between the people making those decisions, a confused picture is likely to emerge – for instance about priorities or about how independent someone is. The decisions taken may even give rise to contradictory solutions, which may actually work against each other. Professionals may also reach different conclusions about which organisation is responsible for providing support.
- **increased risk**. If the professionals who are involved in someone's care do not share information, there may be an aspect of risk that only one person is aware of. Common examples of this relate to the side effects of medication or a person's vulnerability to abuse. Of course, most professionals, doing their job well, will pass on this sort of information; but relying on good practice is less effective than a co-ordinated system where information is automatically shared in the first place. There is also a risk that people will be unable to gain access to services at all, particularly if their needs do not match the way services are structured or they have difficulty communicating.
- **delay**. An unco-ordinated process is likely to result in delays, simply because it takes longer and because it is more likely to require *ad hoc* communication between professionals once they have identified an anomaly in the decisions being made. Disputes about who is responsible for what will also delay matters.

How poorly co-ordinated services affect staff

Staff feel the effects too:

- **inefficient use of time**. When each assessor has to gather information from scratch, they are duplicating the work of other assessors and wasting time that could be spent on more important tasks.
- **filling in the gaps in the system**. Conscientious staff are likely to spend time trying to co-ordinate their activities with others, even if the system is not set up to help them do so.

> ### TRY THIS
>
> ### Identify what changes are needed
>
> After considering the descriptions of difficulties that service users and carers – and also staff – experience when services are not integrated, try to build an analysis of your local services.
>
> What changes do you think will be needed at each of the following levels to achieve the greater integration that might help overcome those difficulties?
> - individual service user
> - service networks
> - the whole system.

- **inter-professional conflict**. A system that does not encourage proper dialogue between professionals at an early stage is more likely to lead to conflicting opinions about the services an individual needs and who is responsible for providing them. If service users and carers are also aware of these conflicting views, they are likely to lose confidence in the professionals.

Improving service outcomes

It is one thing for people to decide that they need greater service integration, but another to discern what this means in practice. One way to clarify what aspects of a service require integration is to consider the *service outcomes* that you are seeking to achieve.

Below we describe four common service outcomes that will be influenced by the extent of integration. For each outcome we have suggested ways in which greater integration could help. We have also given examples, in some of the boxes, of how two of the Health Act flexibilities (pooled budgets and integrated provision) might be used to support integration. The flexibilities should be seen as a means to an end, and used where they will increase the likelihood of improved and integrated outcomes for service users. Do bear in mind that there will be many ways in which integration can be improved without using the flexibilities.

Outcome 1: Service users and their carers have easy access to services without having to know the structures and responsibilities of different organisations

New potential service users are unlikely to know how services are organised or which organisation provides or funds particular services. People whose needs are complex will find it hard to navigate the system, as indeed will the staff who are trying to refer them to the most appropriate service. The larger the number of potential 'doorways', the greater the difficulty.

There are several ways in which integrated services can be used to overcome these problems. One approach is to create a single contact point from which people can be

> **USE OF HEALTH ACT FLEXIBILITIES**
>
> Pooled budgets could be used to fund training for staff at the different access points and to develop a suitable information database for them to use that covers all main services. This could involve a wide range of services including housing, leisure, libraries, community health, GP practices, hospital reception, switchboard staff and voluntary organisations.
>
> Pooled budgets could be used to fund the running costs of joint services such as one-stop shops or customer information services.
>
> Co-location – bringing services physically together – can be made even more effective by bringing them under a single management structure too. With single management, coherent decisions that benefit both staff and users can be made about access to services and the use of space.

directed to the most appropriate service (see box 2a). An example at national level is NHS Direct, a telephone help line that gives information about the best way to respond to health problems. Care Direct is a similar concept that is being developed to meet information needs related to older people's services. On a local level, call centres and one-stop shops also aim to simplify access.

Multiple points of access can be made more user-friendly if you ensure that they provide consistent information to everyone who contacts them. If staff in all access points are trained to the same standard and have the same information about services, policy and systems, users will find the services more 'joined-up'.

The physical co-location of related services is another way to ease access for users, who may then find that the majority of their needs can be met during one visit.

Outcome 2: High quality assessment and re-assessment of a user's needs, that puts the user's needs at the centre, is completed in a timely way and results in a clear care plan
The quality of assessments is a central factor in producing effective outcomes for the people whose needs are being considered. The decisions arising from assessments lead to the allocation of resources, first to the individual and then, on a cumulative basis, to the commissioning budget (see box 2a). There are several ways in which greater integration can improve the assessment process. Here are three.

- Develop an assessment system that requires the involvement of relevant professionals within a set timescale. For example, one of the continuing underlying problems with hospital discharge is the lack of timely and accurate information from all profession-als (e.g. social worker, doctor, nurse, therapist) being fed into assessment. A single

---

USE OF HEALTH ACT FLEXIBILITIES

The introduction of a single assessment process will only be effective if there is joint 'ownership' of the work entailed in establishing, implement-ing and maintaining it.

In some areas, progress on introducing single assessment has been hampered because one organisation had led and funded the work, or because funding has been from short-term pots, causing people to lose confidence that change will really occur. This is a potential area for pooled budgets to cover development costs, training and people's continuing development.

2a. Hammersmith and Fulham: 'Keep Well at Home'

The service covers 20 GP practices that care for half of the borough's population of people aged over 75 years. All over-75s who are on GP lists receive an initial screening, using a validated postal questionnaire. Those assessed as being 'at risk', including all non-responders, are offered an assessment that is carried out using the EasyCare assessment tool. Help is provided with benefits claims, arranging repairs or adaptations, promoting healthy and active lifestyles and encouraging people to be more proactive about contacting services. Many older people who were not previously in touch with services have been identified, and many previously unrecognised problems have been addressed.

Source: *Integrated Services for Older People*, Audit Commission, October 2002

---

protocol or contract that sets out the responsibilities of each professional, with timescales to stick to, could improve the process.

- Adopt a single assessment process for all individuals with complex needs, which is shared between the professionals who contribute to it. This reduces the risk of duplication and encourages a dialogue between those involved that is more likely to lead to an agreement about the outcome of the assessment. When individuals combine mental health or learning disabilities and other needs, the integration of assessment is especially important, because the risk of poor co-ordination is greater.

- Promote prevention through a co-ordinated, proactive approach to screening, assessing and meeting the needs of people at risk (see, for example, box 2a, 'Keep Well at Home'). Integration is essential to this work, as no one sector has the reach or breadth of services required.

Outcome 3: Minimising waits between stages of assessment and care planning
The longer the wait between gathering assessment information and agreeing a care plan, the greater the risk that information will be out of date and that users and carers and others will be frustrated. It is possible to develop assessment systems that minimise the waits between stages of assessment and care planning. For instance, one person can be given responsibility for co-ordinating the assessment process and ensuring that progress is maintained, or authority to agree the funding of a care plan can be given to the person who has made the assessment and suggested that plan: when a care manager role is created and given this authority, then a significant cause of delay is removed.

Waits can also be reduced by establishing teams that work across domains, for example teams of social work, health and housing staff who work between hospital and the community and do not have to pass assessments on to new teams and risk delays (see box 2b).

Outcome 4: High quality services that promote maximum independence and quality of life for users and their carers and are flexible enough to reflect changing needs
The quality of services provided depends on a combination of micro-commissioning – i.e. organising services to meet an individual's needs – and macro-commissioning – i.e.

USE OF HEALTH ACT FLEXIBILITIES

Multi-disciplinary teams working across domains will have the greatest chance of success if they are within a single management structure and working to common protocols.

2b: Integrating the Care Programme Approach (CPA) and care management

In Bedfordshire, Haringey, Hounslow and Leicester the CPA and social services care management have been integrated into a single system for assessment, care planning and review.

Source: *Modernising Mental Health Services*, Social Services Inspectorate, DoH, June 2002

purchasing services to meet the needs of the wider population. The quality and flexibility of services can be increased in various ways, including:

- providing direct payments to individuals to enable them to buy services to meet their needs. This enables people to integrate their own services. LAs can increase the success of this approach by helping people to set up packages of care and by managing the local market for community-based services in a way that promotes quality and flexibility.
- developing multi-agency, multi-disciplinary intermediate care services that provide people with the best possible opportunities to maintain or regain independence. An example is a rapid response, out-of-hours service that provides:
  - immediate support at home for 24 hours until assessment and other services can be arranged
  - out-of-hours advice and support, and referral if necessary
  - up to six weeks of rehabilitation and recuperation support, at home or in a special facility
  - assessment of accident and emergency attendees for their potential to be discharged, with support.
- having a commissioning strategy that integrates quality and flexibility at the micro level, with well thought out contracts and specifications to determine what is commissioned at a macro level (see box 2c). To make this work, you need to set up a system where the perspectives of service users and carers and front-line staff help to determine the overall commissioning of services.

What service integration cannot achieve

The flexibilities can be used in relation to any 'health related' function of local government, and therefore a lot can be included. For example, the flexibilities will allow the integration of education, health and social care for children, and integrated services including housing, environmental services, refuse collection, special transport and leisure.

However, an integrated service will be part of a larger network of services and there will always be services 'outside' it that it will need to be linked to. For example, a rapid response team for older people would need effective links with the following services, (assuming they were not included within it): the primary health care team; diagnostic services, e.g. x-ray, blood tests; a community geriatrician; specialist medical input, e.g. neurology, orthopaedics; transport; equipment; housing adaptations; and day care or the hospital.

Integration will not resolve underlying conflicts or a lack of trust between organisations. Without trust and genuine consultation, partnerships are unlikely to be successful. If co-operation between services has failed in the past, then you will need to explore the reasons why before making any moves towards integration.

Care trusts

Since the Health Act was published, many organisations have felt that they must choose between implementing the flexibilities and setting up a care trust. A major concern for NHS bodies and LAs is whether, by opting for one or more of the flexibilities, they will make it more difficult to move to a care trust in the future. The key difference between the two options is that care trusts are all embracing, whilst the flexibilities are likely to be applied only to some services. However, they have the same underlying themes of integrating the planning, purchasing and provision of services, and are not mutually exclusive. Groundwork done towards implementing flexibilities will pave the way for care trusts.

Probably the most fruitful way to consider these issues is to look at the purpose of any new way of working and the factors that will make flexibilities and care trust compatible.

USE OF HEALTH ACT FLEXIBILITIES

Flexible services should respond to changing user needs, such as an acute episode within a long-term condition or an increase in dependency. Users and carers also want flexible services, for example transport that can pick them up at different times, or help to go to bed later than usual. If pooled budgets are delegated to front-line staff, they can purchase services more quickly and flexibly.

If commissioning budgets are also pooled, there will be far greater potential to influence a range of providers to develop more integrated and flexible services. For example, housing, social services, transport and health might want to commission an integrated equipment service to meet needs in people's own homes, including sheltered housing, residential or nursing homes and clinics. The equipment might include wheelchairs, special transport, special beds and mattresses, moving and handling equipment and alarm systems.

Using a pooled budget to employ staff within an integrated service would enable the manager of the service to get the most appropriate mix of skills within his or her staff group. Pooled budgets to cover staffing costs will be most effective in combination with integrated provision, because one manager will control the recruitment, terms and conditions and training of staff.

The nature of intermediate care services is that they involve different professionals working across traditional organisational barriers, often with an imperative to move quickly. Bringing these services within one management structure is likely to improve the prospects for aligning practice and providing a streamlined service.

2c. Recommissioning mental health services in Hammersmith and Fulham

A specialist independent sector domiciliary support service has recently been commissioned for people on the Care Programme Approach. This service attends to the practicalities of users' lives and could work alongside them in cooking, cleaning, budgeting, personal care and gardening. Two workers concentrate on preventing hospital admissions by working on accommodation and welfare benefits.

Source: *Modernising Mental Health Services*, Social Services Inspectorate, DoH, June 2002

The things that will make a difference to services users and carers will be:

- the use of common assessment systems for health and social care needs.
- improved co-ordination and integration of services where duplication, gaps and discontinuity otherwise occur.
- faster responses from services, especially for people at risk.
- involving people more in decisions.
- more integrated and accessible information systems for individual care and service planning.
- services that promote independence and prevent deterioration.
- intermediate care services that enable people to stay in their own homes.

Things that make the flexibilities and care trusts potentially compatible include:

- incentives to focus on the reality of individual needs without having to distinguish 'health' and 'social' needs (pooled budgets and care trusts).
- encouragement to work co-operatively with other professionals and increase the compatibility of policy and practice (integrated provision and care trusts)
- coherent decisions about the direction in which services are being developed and about priorities in the allocation of resources (lead commissioning and care trusts).
- the potential to use resources more efficiently by reducing duplication (all three flexibilities and care trusts).

> ## TRY THIS
>
> ## Evaluating proposed service integrations
>
> Service integration is often seen as self-evidently a good thing. It is not. Like all innovations, it needs to be checked out to see if it will really result in the gains you seek.
>
> Check out any proposed innovations by examining:
> - outcomes – describing how the independence and quality of life of users and carers will be enhanced.
> - service user experience – checking whether the following are problems and, if so, how it is proposed to tackle them: difficult to access services; the duplication of activities; contradictory decisions; multiple assessments and care plans; increased risks; and delays.
> - service efficiency – checking whether there are problems with the following and, if so, how it is proposed to tackle them: inefficient use of staff time; staff having to fill gaps in the system; and inter-professional conflict.

> ## TRY THIS
>
> ## Wider service integration
>
> It would be neither possible nor desirable to include in one organisation all the services that a particular service user group requires. However, if services are to be user-centred, the integration of all services must still be achieved. Decide how this should be realised by:
> - Choosing a group of service users and considering which services are, or should be integrated by: • organisational mergers; • other means.
> - For the services you think should be integrated by 'other means', evaluate the effectiveness of their current integration and consider what changes might be required at the levels of:
>   - • individual service users   • service networks   • the whole system.

Chapter three: Commissioning

'Commissioning' describes arrangements for obtaining suitable services to meet people's needs. Commissioning takes place at the three operational levels we have described already: individual service users; service networks; and the whole system.

At the level of the individual service user, commissioning involves organising a package of services for one person or family. At the service network level, there can be arrangements (sometimes in the form of contracts) for providing services to cover a geographical area and/or a particular group of users. Commissioning at the level of whole systems, markets and economies involves planning and funding services to meet the needs of large groups of people or whole populations. At any of these three levels, commissioning may involve the allocation of existing services, 'call-off' from an existing contract or the use of cash to purchase new services.

The history of co-operation in commissioning

It has long been recognised that the NHS and social services are often providing support to the same individuals or families, as well as having responsibility for the same overall population. It is not surprising, then, that there have been a number of attempts to develop greater co-ordination in setting priorities and directing resources.

We can find examples of health and social services developing co-operative approaches to commissioning activities over the last 20 years: the development of joint teams in mental health and learning disability is one such example, designed to make the assessment of need and planning of care more consistent. However, these developments have not always led to the extent of integration that people had hoped for. In the last ten years, two approaches – the 'care programme approach' (CPA) in mental health and 'single assessment' for older people's services – have aimed at minimising differences in practices between professions.

At the whole system level, there is a long history of attempts at joint planning, such as the joint care planning teams, where staff from health and local government would meet to discuss their priorities for local services development. These systems had access to modest, time-limited funds called 'joint finance' that could be used for important joint priorities, but on the whole, joint strategic planning has suffered from the fact that most plans are led either by health or by local government and that resources have been managed separately.

Prior to the Health Act, 1999, there were attempts to encourage what was described as 'joint commissioning', where strategic commissioning activities would be undertaken in an integrated fashion. Although progress was made in some areas, there were difficulties establishing legally acceptable arrangements without creating entirely new bodies to take on commissioning. This led to increased pressure from health and social care to change legislation, resulting in Section 31 of the Health Act.

Part of the difficulty with joint planning and commissioning is that health and social care bodies organise and understand the commissioning process differently. It is worth taking a look at these differences.

Commissioning social care

In social services, the legacy from the Community Care Act is the description of assessment and care planning for people as 'purchasing' or 'commissioning'. This is distinct from service 'provision', and it is usually managed separately too. The reasoning behind this separation is that decisions about what care someone receives should be free from the influence of the people providing it. It was also seen as putting council providers and independent sector providers on a more level playing field.

Care managers who assess needs and organise care are separate from the staff who provide home care or work in residential care. The care manager's role is therefore seen as commissioning because, having decided that certain services are needed, he or she will go ahead and secure services to meet the needs. The care manager – or their manager – has the power either to refer a person to their own authority's social care services or to purchase independent sector care, using the budget allocated for commissioning.

At the service network level, various commissioning arrangements exist. Where social services have their own residential or home care services, the funding to these services is provided annually. Depending on council policy, funding may be linked to detailed service specifications and SLAs or to something less formal.

Some SSDs have transferred much of their residential and home care into the independent sector, from which they purchase services, using legally binding contracts based on service specifications. These contracts may be handled by staff in social services or through a central contract unit. Many of these are so-called 'spot' contracts, where a specific contract is drawn up relating to the needs of an individual. Spot contracts are most often used to purchase residential and nursing home places, because they allow flexibility in the choice of home and avoid the risk of funding empty places.

Social services also enter into what are called 'block' contracts, which enable them to buy care for several people from one provider. Block contracts are most often used to purchase home care, because the number of people needing care is greater than those needing residential care and it is possible to build flexibility into the package arranged for each individual. As major purchasers of independent sector services, LAs have considerable potential to influence their local market for care.

The social services budget is part of the wider council budget and so is subject to competition for funds with other council services. At a whole system level, social services will usually divide its budgets between client groups – e.g. older people, children, people with learning disabilities – to reflect competing demands on services and plans for development. Increasingly, discussions about future service planning and funding take place in multi-agency forums, as described above in the paragraph on the history of co-operation in commissioning.

Like health, social care is part of the overall community planning process orchestrated by the LA on behalf of the local strategic partnership (LSP). Being able to show how proposals fit with the local community plan is a requirement, across all sectors, for the receipt of a significant amount of central government funding. It is through the LSP and its sub-partnerships that health and social care are supposed to co-ordinate their strategies, shape policy and obtain funding in areas such as community safety, lifelong learning and regeneration.

Commissioning health care

In health care, assessing need and planning care for individuals are usually part and parcel of service provision. Nurses, therapists and doctors assess need and provide care directly. Within a hospital or community setting, a number of professionals may be involved in providing care. Access to this care is determined through systems like waiting lists, risk assessment and emergency needs. Occasionally, health staff might undertake an assessment and decide that someone needs a service that can only or best be provided outside the local health services. For example, clinicians might be involved in assessing someone with complex health needs who will be referred to services outside the area. However, the budgets for funding any referrals to outside services are usually held at a senior level.

General practitioners (GPs) also assess needs, provide direct care and refer people to other services. They do not hold budgets with which to purchase care.

Until April 2002, HAs undertook the commissioning of health care for their local population as a whole, using funds they received from the Department of Health (DoH). The role of HAs was to agree with providers (mainly hospitals and community health services) what would be provided, and funds were transferred on the basis of block contracts for certain levels of activity.

In April 2002, the commissioning role of HAs transferred to PCTs. At the same time, general community health services (usually excluding mental health and learning disabilities) came under the direct management of PCTs, effectively making these PCT 'in-house' services. For example, PCTs will manage district nurses, community therapists, school nurses, dieticians, health visitors and continence advisors. Acute hospitals and specialist health trusts that provide mental health and learning disability services remain independent of PCTs, which commission services from them.

When PCTs were established, the mechanism for commissioning from acute hospitals and specialist trusts was supposed to be through SLAs, although progress in replacing block contracts with SLAs was very slow. In November 2002, the DoH published details of a new system, be introduced gradually, for PCTs to use to commission acute services. This will involve the allocation of money, linked to SLAs, with nationally set prices (tariffs) for specific services. In the first instance, this system will be introduced for elective care, that is, pre-planned care involving specific clinical procedures, such as surgery. A key difference between this system of commissioning and the current one is the potential for PCTs to withdraw funds from providers during the financial year if it is clear that targets for acute services will not be met.

PCTs also ensure the provision of primary health care. They are responsible for overseeing the quality of services provided by GPs and other members of primary health care teams.

The implications for integration

Integration between health and social care at the **individual** (or family) level is likely to involve people who have different experiences of commissioning. For example, at this level, you might find social work care managers, GPs and district nurses all involved, taking an integrated approach to the assessment of individual need and arranging care (see box 3a). Of the three, only the care managers might have access to a cash budget to buy services and prior experience of negotiating with providers. District nurses may only have control over

3a. Halton: GP-based, joint case management

A GP practice in Runcorn, along with the social services department, piloted a joint case management approach to reducing admissions and the length of hospital stays among older people. The project concentrated on people who were at high risk of hospital admission, or who were making heavy use of the service. The care management nurse would contact people at risk to assess their needs. Follow-up could include health education, practical advice or referral to other services, many of which were low-level, community-based support services provided by voluntary organisations. The number of admissions and the average length of stay both fell. Links between practice staff and other agencies improved and there were more appropriate referrals and much faster response times for social services assessments.

Source: *Integrated Services for Older People*, Audit Commission, October 2002

the allocation of their own time, and GPs, apart from allocating their own time, may have to refer an individual to NHS services that are defined within an overall PCT contract. If integration is going to be effective, there will need to be agreement between them all about the ways in which each partner secures services, and a common understanding of the constraints on choice and flexibility under which each works.

At the **service network** level, too, there are differences in commissioning capacity. Taking the example of intermediate care services for older people, it is possible to identify some of the issues. When deciding what model of care to provide, social services might decide to adapt some of its own home care services and to contract with a residential care provider to offer short-term rehabilitation beds. The PCT, on the other hand, may find it harder to ensure that complementary NHS services are in place. If part of the intermediate care service is nurses and therapists working in hospital to offer early rehabilitation and assessment, the PCT needs to find 'levers' for negotiating new ways of working with the hospital (see box 3b). To make all these links work well, the service network will require overall co-ordination, often at a locality level.

At the **whole system** level, the integration of different organisations' strategic plans requires an ability to ensure that resources are directed in a co-ordinated way. Partner organisations need to understand the nature and extent of influence that they each have over the market for care (see box 3c). For example, although social services purchase considerable amounts of independent care, the use of spot contracts for care home places can deter providers from taking risks about developing new services, because there is no guarantee of long-term, reliable income.

3b. Leeds: Joint care management teams

Established in 2000 and now based in the PCTs, joint care management teams in Leeds comprise nurses, therapists, social welfare assistants and social workers who have been relocated from hospital social work teams. The joint teams will follow older people's progress when they go into hospital, track them through the system, make sure they return home as early as possible, and manage risk appropriately.

Source: *Integrated Services for Older People*, Audit Commission, October 2002

3c. Brighton and Hove: Domiciliary care market

Looking into a shortage of domiciliary care workers, the council commissioned an independent study of recruitment across all sectors. This highlighted the need to provide more stability for local businesses and to introduce better terms and conditions of service across the sectors. The study informed the council's commissioning strategy. It raised its fees, offered enhancements for service users requiring intensive or specialist care and appointed 'approved providers' for different geographical areas to guarantee minimum levels of business, while maintaining a competitive market across the city as a whole.

Source: *Tracking the Changes*, Joint Reviews, Audit Commission, 2002

Aligning existing commissioning processes

If integrated commissioning is to produce the desired benefits, existing processes will need to be modified or linked.

List the commissioning processes used in health and in social care at each of the following levels:
- individual service users
- service networks
- the whole system

Identify how they are integrated and whether any further integration is required.

Individuals purchasing their own care

Some people purchase their own care services because they have sufficient funds to do so and are able to arrange services without assistance from statutory health and social care organisations. They may purchase acute or community health care, places in nursing and residential care homes, home care or therapy services. In some cases, the money will come from social security benefits, such as attendance allowance.

As we noted in chapter one, it is now possible for people to be offered 'direct payments' by social services: sums of money with which to purchase care for themselves. Having received the payment, the person selects the care he or she wants, negotiates with the provider and agrees a contract. Where such schemes have been developed, it is common to offer the person some initial support with the process, particularly with aspects such as employing care workers. There is no reason, in principle, why these schemes should not expand considerably, and national policy is starting to encourage this by requiring LAs to offer direct payments as an option to all service users.

The implications for integration

If substantial numbers of service users take up the option of direct payments, the role of commissioners at the **individual user** level will need to change. Indeed, commissioners may make a positive decision to move in this direction in order to *enable* users to have greater control over their care. Demand for direct care management will lessen, while the need for information and help with decisions about how and what to purchase will increase.

At the **service network** level, funds previously used to commission external services will be directed to users, and this will reduce the budgets for direct commissioning. Also, the professionals who come into contact with individual users will need to ensure that information and support is provided in a co-ordinated way, to enable people to find out about direct payments and make best use of them if they choose this route.

If more people take up the option of direct payments then, at the **whole system** level, the balance of direct commissioning and market management will also change. As we described earlier, LAs, and occasionally the NHS, will purchase care from independent sector providers; often these will be providers from which self-funding individuals will also be purchasing services. Commissioners have an interest in influencing the overall supply of a service and its quality, because the availability of these services will be part of the strategic commissioning plan. They have obligations, too, to their local communities to promote health. The types of influence that commissioners may wish to take an integrated approach to include: negotiating good standards of service that affect everyone who receives them; providing information to the community to help them make choices about care, whether through self funding or not; and finding out about the size and composition of the self-funding part of the market, to identify the effect of demand on cost and quality.

> ## TRY THIS
>
> ## Managing the large-scale use of direct payments
>
> If, in your locality, 10 per cent of the individual older people for whom social services provide assessment and care management switched to direct payments:
> - can you estimate how much money would be taken out of the commissioning budget?
> - what new skills and knowledge would be needed, and by whom?
> - how would you influence the development of the independent sector?

Integrating commissioning in health and social care

Despite the differences between health and social care described above, the basic tasks for each service are the same, although they may be carried out in different places. Once again, they can be seen operating at the three levels:

- **individual service users**: assessing need, planning and purchasing care for individuals with complex needs
- **service networks**: monitoring and managing contracts and service agreements within a locality or across a specialist service network
- the **whole system**: strategic planning, commissioning and market management for the whole population or service user groups.

> ## 3d. Conwy: Integrated assessment and care management teams
>
> The Elderly Care and Assessment Team and the Care Management and Assessment Rehabilitation Team were set up as joint ventures between Conwy and the Denbighshire NHS Trust. They work in similar ways in different localities to prevent unnecessary admissions to acute hospitals, facilitate early discharge, help prevent unnecessary placements in residential and nursing homes and enable people to live in their own homes. Indications are that the teams are reducing emergency intakes, ensuring that people can remain self-supporting after discharge from hospital and reducing the use of nursing and residential home provision.
>
> Source: *Pathways to Improved Social Services in Wales,* Joint Reviews, Audit Commission, Oct. 2002

The benefits of integration

There are benefits to integrating activities across organisations at any of the three levels. The benefits relate to reduced duplication of work and greater consistency in decision making.

For example:

- if the assessment of need is integrated at the **individual service user** level, a person or family being supported by several services will be asked less often for information, staff will not have to collect information that others have already collected and the risk of two professionals reaching contradictory decisions will be reduced (see box 3d).

3e. Rotherham: Community assessment and treatment service

A programme of services has been established to prevent hospital admission and to promote independence. It has a number of components.

- A fast response service providing short periods of nursing and social care in the community
- Broom Hays residential unit, providing intensive functional rehabilitation for a maximum of six weeks
- Millennium rehabilitation day unit, providing therapy for a maximum of six weeks
- Nurse-led beds purchased for a maximum of 14 days in local nursing homes for low-key rehabilitation and recovery.

Some of the strengths of this system are that:

- service users like the service and feel they are receiving appropriate help to remain independent
- integrated working is happening between health and social services, using mainstream funding.

Source: *Improving Older People's Services*, Social Services Inspectorate, DoH, October 2002

- if co-ordinated services are being commissioned at the **service networks** level, the agreements commissioners make with providers can require them to co-operate with other providers (see box 3e). In managing their local service networks, commissioners have to make sure that the contracted supply of services actually meets the needs of all service users, including those who are self-funding.
- at the **whole system** level, integrated strategic planning enables resources to be concentrated on joint priorities, and consistent messages to be given to the public about intentions and outcomes. It also provides opportunities for local government to make certain that the role of services such as housing, education and environment are included in plans (see box 3f). Co-operation in developing contracts and service agreements will reduce the risk of unhelpful competition over pricing or terms and conditions.

3f. Bolton: Better government for older people

Following on from being a pilot project, Bolton has identified an 'older person's champion' at executive member level, appointed an older people's services co-ordinator and involved older people on the policy development group. It expects every council department to produce action plans.

Source: 'Tracking the Changes', Joint Reviews, Audit Commission, 2002

Horizontal and vertical integration

Very often, you discover there is a lack of integration at each of the three levels *within* sectors. When this is so, it may be more difficult to integrate activities *between* sectors. For example, if social services uses several different assessment systems for adults, integrating the health and social care assessment processes will be more complicated. It is important, therefore, to give proper consideration to what potential there is to integrate both within and between sectors. Table 3.1, overleaf, illustrates what we have called 'horizontal integration', i.e. the integration of each level of activity across organisations. The left hand column shows what integration looks like within health, the middle shows integration within social care and the right hand column shows integration across organisations.

The ultimate aim of the commissioning process is to obtain services that meet people's needs most effectively and efficiently. We have talked several times about the three levels at which commissioning operates (individual service user, service networks and the whole system). Although these can be seen as distinct, they need to be closely linked if the whole commissioning system is to produce effective outcomes for service users. The overall strategy at the whole system level needs to shape the service specifications and contracts being used at the service network level. At the individual level, information about both the quality and the appropriateness of services needs to be collected and fed back into the monitoring of contracts at the network

---

TRY THIS

How integrated is your assessment system?

How many separate sets of records could your organisation hold about a single person?

If a partner organisation came to you and asked about your assessment system for older people, would you be able to show them one single set of procedures?

3g. Strategic planning

Bromley – a National Service Framework co-ordinator is jointly funded by health and social services. There is an NSF action plan and a sub-group that reports to the Older Person's Partnership Board, which is the joint planning and commissioning agency.

Camden – plans are in place for most services to adults to be provided jointly by social services and health, and made available through the two PCTs.

Devon – plans are in place to arrange and provide mental health services and services for people with leaning disabilities jointly with health partners.

Rochdale – integrated approaches to providing services for older people and people with learning disabilities have been established.

Southwark – a multi-agency Community Care Executive Board implements the Joint Investment Plan, the NSF and the NHS Plan.

Sources:
(1) *Improving Older People's Services*, Social Services Inspectorate, DoH, October 2002;
(2) *Modernising Services to Improve Care*, Social Services Inspectorate, DoH, June 2002

table 3.1 Some examples of the horizontal integration of commissioning			
	INTEGRATION WITHIN HEALTH SERVICES	INTEGRATION WITHIN SOCIAL CARE	INTEGRATION ACROSS SECTORS
INDIVIDUAL SERVICE USER	• Single assessment process and link worker or care manager • Process is used by all professionals within a service area e.g. older people's services	• Single assessment process and link worker or care manager • Process applies to services for different groups e.g. older people, mental health, physical disability	• Single assessment process and care manager across sectors for specific user groups. (these are referred to as a 'care programme approach' for mental health; and a 'person centred approach' for learning disability) • Single record across sectors
SERVICE NETWORKS	• Care pathway co-ordination between primary care and community nursing to prevent hospital admission and with the acute sector to enable discharge	• Care management and domiciliary care teams work to jointly agreed priorities to support people at risk	• Pooled budget for purchasing care packages, agreed joint priorities and processes between care management, primary care, community nursing teams and local service providers; co-ordinated by a lead network manager
WHOLE SYSTEM	• PCT agrees a single specification with several providers (acute, community, primary care) for one type of service • PCT joins with other PCT(s) to commission service • PCTs across an area plan jointly	• Social services arranges a single contract for services to several user groups e.g. home care • Best value performance plan for whole LA area shows how different groups of service users will benefit from improvements across all LA services	• One organisation is the lead commissioner and has access to the pooled budget for funding the contracts • Contracts require different providers to work co-operatively to provide a co-ordinated service • Joint work on managing the market for health and social care e.g. influencing pay rates, developing affordable housing, increasing in-area provision • Partnership boards for a whole service area that agree objectives to guide the use of resources (see box 3g) • Participation in LSP is based on the community strategy that incorporates regeneration and broad public health

level. It should also be used to influence the way service networks are managed, the commissioning of services and the overall strategic plan.

This flow of information between the levels of commissioning activity needs to be systematic and it needs to be constant, because the patterns of need will not remain the same over time.

We have described this integration as 'vertical'. Table 3.2 illustrates the features that might exist in a system where the three types of commissioning are linked vertically.

table 3.2 Some examples of the vertical integration of commissioning		
	INTEGRATION WITHIN HEALTH SERVICES	INTEGRATION WITHIN SOCIAL CARE	INTEGRATION ACROSS SECTORS
INDIVIDUAL SERVICE USER / SERVICE NETWORKS / WHOLE SYSTEM	• Information about patients' needs and referral routes is aggregated to show how demand for health care is changing. • Information about patients' views and clinical outcomes is collected to show how well providers are performing. This feeds into PCT decisions about SLAs. • Network management priorities are adjusted to handle shifts in demand. • Information is collected about use of services and waiting times to determine whether there is over- or under-provision. • Differences in priority demand between service networks influence overall resource allocation.	• Information about user perceptions of quality is collected as part of quality assurance. • Information from assessments is aggregated to show trends in demand and profiles of users e.g. age, ethnicity, gender, residence. • Simple, easy-to-use systems exist for front-line staff and users to report failures in service: useful for negotiations with providers. • Users' perceptions of social care providers' services inform service network level contract management. • Users and front-line staff are involved in the development of service specifications. • Quality and contract management issues are taken into account in the recommissioning of services.	• Agreement exists on which groups of users to gather information about and what information to collect. • Common systems exist for collecting information. • Users and front-line staff are consulted jointly about their experience of services, with a particular focus on aspects of integration. • Pooled budgets and integrated management introduced to improve co-ordination at local service and individual level. • Lead commissioning is informed by the shifting picture of needs, local service network management responses and the use of pooled budgets.

The implications for organisations

We have argued that decisions cannot be taken about systems at one level in isolation from the others. Connections need to be established that enable the flow of information between levels and influence decisions. For example, if you introduce single assessment for older people, your strategic planning needs to use the information from those assessments to inform long-term

TRY THIS

Vertical integration

Identify a new development in integrated working that you wish to introduce, for example intermediate care or integrated assessments.

Use table 3.2 to evaluate what may be needed, within each sector and cross-sector, to support the integration through changes at the levels of:
• the individual service user
• service networks
• the whole system.

planning. Equally, the SLAs and contracts for services need to contain a requirement to use single assessment and to collate information on needs at the service network level.

In the next chapter, we look at the next crucial component of successful integration: involving the people who make use of services and who will benefit from the improved outcomes you are trying to achieve.

Chapter four: Involving patients, service users, carers and the public

A central idea in service integration is that of working back from the outcomes that service users want to see, in order to develop the systems that will enable these outcomes to be realised. If service integration is to be effective, it is essential that the voices of users and carers, and those of the general public, are heard and taken into account in both the re-organisation of services and their continued management. This requires a dialogue at each of the three levels of integration:

individual service user level – ensuring individual patients, service users and their carers have a say in the services they receive and the way these operate

service networks level – responding to individual comments and complaints about the way particular local organisations and service networks operate, and involving patients, service users and carers in managing the performance of these organisations and networks

the **whole system** level – involving patients, service users and carers in the development of overall strategies for health and social care, setting priorities and implementing them. This also means taking a wider view of people's needs, encompassing not just health and social care but other relevant services too. It means involving patients, service users and carers in the development and shaping of the markets and economies for health, home and residential care, transport and housing.

Ways of involving service users, patients, carers and the public

Health and social care managers and professionals, and LAs as a whole, have developed different approaches to involving people in decisions about their care. New legislation and policy developments have begun a further wave of transformation. We outline these below.

Health

The Health and Social Care Act, 2001 and the DoH policy document *Involving Patients and the Public in Healthcare* are bringing in a completely new set of arrangements for involving patients and the public in health services themselves and in tackling the determinants of health inequalities. Previously, attempts to involve patients and members of the public in health were limited to community health councils, complaints procedures, some advocacy services and a few discussions about plans and major reconfigurations of services.

The new arrangements are designed to work at three linked levels: locally through NHS trusts and LAs; strategically with SHAs; and nationally. At each level, the aim is to bring together the ideas of patients and the public, NHS bodies and LA elected members. The main elements will be:

- **Patients Advice and Liaison Services** (PALS). Employed by, and responsible to, local NHS trusts, PALS will provide patients with on-the-spot help, resolve problems, inform patients of complaints procedures and link them to independent advocacy services. They will monitor and report problems to trusts and patients forums. The intention is for them to operate in a network with other PALS services in their area to provide a 'seamless' service to patients.

- **Independent Complaints Advocacy Services** (ICAS). Independent of the NHS, and commissioned locally by the new Commission for Patient and Public Involvement in Health (CPPIH), these new advocacy services will complement and support existing ones such as the current mental health advocacy services.

- **patients forums**. These will be set up in each NHS trust and PCT, with members appointed through a CPPIH process designed to make sure that they are representative of all groups, including socially excluded groups. A forum's responsibilities will include inspecting the health services provided by the trust, GPs and the independent sector, from the patient's perspective. The results of its reviews of these services, as well as of the complaints procedures and the PALS and ICAS services, will be used by the trust to inform and influence management decision making. One of the trust's non-executive board members will be elected from the patients forum, and the forum will report annually to the trust, the LA overview and scrutiny committee, local MPs, the SHA, CPPIH and the National Patient Safety Agency (NPSA).

- **LA overview and scrutiny committees**. Comprising non-executive elected members, these committees scrutinise both local NHS provision – including the roles played by PCTs and the SHA – and the joint LA-health responsibility for improving health and reducing health inequalities. They have the power to refer public concerns about major changes in local health services or instances of inadequate consultation with local people to the Secretary of State.

- **Commission for Patient and Public Involvement in Health (CPPIH).** The Commission is an independent body operating at national, strategic and local levels. Nationally, it researches examples of good practice and identifies, sets and publishes quality standards for ICAS, PALS and patients forums. It employs local networks of staff to commission ICAS services and it delivers its findings, including an annual report, to the Secretary of State for Health, CHI, professional regulatory bodies, NPSA and the Health Select Committee. At the strategic level, CPPIH's local staff aggregate local findings and channel them through the SHA and centrally to CPPIH. Locally, it focuses on health 'determinants' as well as health care, feeding its findings into LAs' community leadership responsibilities and community development activities. Among its other local responsibilities are: commissioning ICAS services; providing administrative and networking support to patients forums; and informing the work of LA overview and scrutiny committees. CPPIH's work priorities are guided by a lay reference panel that includes representatives from patients forums and the LSP.

Social care

The introduction of community care planning in the 1990s also saw an acceleration in the development of self-help and self-representation groups of service users and their carers, and advocacy services. These groups and services focused on both health and social care, and often on other related services too. Some of this development was financially supported by grants from LAs. This led to the development of forums of service users and carers that facilitated the exchange of views between different groups and were useful as vehicles for consulting people. At the same time, user representation on joint planning groups and in the actual work of developing social care services became more common. In some areas, user and carer groups have regular formal and informal contact with elected members.

The measurement of users' satisfaction with services is one of a number of people-focused 'indicators' (or measures) used in the joint reviews of SSDs by the Audit Commission and the SSI.

Local authorities

In the 1990s, LAs began to introduce new approaches to finding out what members of the public thought and involving them in decision making. We saw the emergence of:

- **citizens panels** – representative groups of local people who agree to be polled regularly or to participate in focus groups to give their views on local issues and service developments.
- **citizens juries** – small, representative groups of local people who agree to work together for a fixed period on an issue of local concern, calling local and external 'expert witnesses', weighing the evidence and making recommendations for action.
- **area committees or forums** – sometimes these are formal sub-committees of elected members, with a small delegated budget; in other places they are panels of officers and members, who act as sounding boards and regularly report to the local people of a defined geographical area.
- **best value** – consultation with all interested parties, including service users and the general public, is a required part of a best value review. The move away from service-

focused reviews to cross-cutting reviews will mean more focus on broad issues such as health inequalities and their determining factors.

- **scrutiny**. LAs are required to scrutinise both NHS services and the joint responsibility of the LA and health organisations to promote health and well-being. In doing so, they must take into account the views of service users and the general public.
- **partnerships**. 'Action zones', regeneration projects and other neighbourhood renewal projects are usually required to find ways of involving members of the public in their work, as are partnerships working on topics of concern, such as community safety.
- **local strategic partnerships**. An LSP is an umbrella organisation intended to bring together the concerns and aspirations of all local people and to co-ordinate the activities of the partnerships in the local area. An LSP needs to make sure that it consults members of the public when it is working on its community strategy.

How effective are you at involving people locally?

To judge whether any set of activities to involve people is effective, you have first to be sure what it is designed to achieve.

In the case of service improvements, the point of involving local people is to ensure that you provide better, more effective, integrated services and tackle the main issues of concern to patients, service users and carers. Keep this at the front of your thoughts when you are judging the effectiveness of your efforts to involve people.

A clear definition of what counts as an 'improved service' will come from a good understanding of the experiences of users, and of their priorities. When you agree this with users and carers themselves, you will more readily be able to apply it to the services you provide.

Good involvement will help organisations to respond when things go wrong, acknowledge their mistakes, apologise and come up with a solution that meets people's needs. It will also help professionals to behave better towards users and carers. Indeed, the fact that patients, service users and carers are being seen as equal partners in assessing needs, planning care, and deciding how services should operate is an explicit acknowledgement of the major part they can play in improving services.

You will also see improvements in the way your organisation operates. As users, carers and the public help to shape services, they can see their ideas being transformed into practice. A well thought out process for involving people will mean

> EXAMPLES OF LOCAL 'INVOLVEMENT', 'CONSULTATION' OR 'ENGAGEMENT' PROCESSES OR ACTIVITIES.
> - public surveys and questionnaires
> - public meetings
> - councillors' surgeries
> - citizens panels
> - citizens juries
> - surveys of patients and users
> - area committees or forums
> - best value consultation
> - local people's involvement in scrutiny committees, partnerships and LSPs

that decision making and timetables – and the rationale behind them – will be public, explained in non-technical terms and kept up to date. Management activities will be well linked or integrated. Planning will be linked to commissioning and allocating resources, so that the involvement of users and carers in planning naturally affects the rest of the decision making steps. During external inspections, central government will be kept informed of the views and priorities of users and carers, which can also be fed into national lobbying activity.

Most important, improvements in existing services and new service developments will actually come about, and have a substantial basis in the suggestions that users and carers have made.

The process of involving people itself should be designed around users and carers first and organisations second. It should be a seamless, integrated set of activities that is easy to understand and use and is accountable to everyone. Complaints procedures will be well signposted, easy to use and supported by advocacy. People will know where to turn when things go wrong and will be able to expect an integrated, positive response.

Good involvement is democratically accountable and broadly representative of all groups, including those who are socially excluded, so you should aim to use a wide range of activities and techniques to ensure you really do allow all groups to get involved. Also, users do not want to be consulted on the same question over and over again by different organisations; nor do they want to be consulted and then not see any action. Therefore, a well-thought out, integrated process will be such that people are only consulted once on any one subject. It will maintain a broad agenda but also focus on a few priorities and do them well. And it will work from the agenda set by users and carers themselves.

TRY THIS

Making the total pattern of involvement work for service users and the public

The wide variety of 'involvement' or 'engagement' activities that we have mentioned could either provide a rich and effective mixture or be a disconnected set of arrangements that service users and the public just find exhausting to use. To get the best out of existing and evolving arrangements, try this:

- Bring together a representative group of patients, service users and carers, with staff who have been working on patient, user and carer involvement in health, social care and across the LA
- Draw up a 'map' of the involvement processes that you currently use and plan to use to help achieve integrated adult health and social care.
- Select some examples of cross-sector integrations that patients, service users and carers see as being critical – integrated assessments, for example. Examine each one to see how far your involvement activities are helping service users ensure that organisations get their acts together.

What does this tell you about any changes that you might need to make?

Table 4 provides a fictional example to illustrate how you might check how well an organisation is managing to involve people in integrated provision. The organisation portrayed is certainly making an effort, but falling down in some respects.

What table 4 shows us, (using each of the three levels of integration):

- **individual service user**. Service users are involved in assessing their own needs and in planning care. However, in this example, the impact of their involvement is weakened by the lack of a co-ordinated or integrated assessment process. So these service users still have to work too hard to get integrated action.
- **service networks**. The range of activities, both within and across health and social care, pick up the views of service users on how well service networks are working. In this example, however, service users are not involved in the monthly performance management meetings of the local service networks and so their views have little influence.
- the **whole system**. There is a long history of consulting people about overall strategies for health and social care services. However the means by which strategies

table 4: Checking how far the involvement of patients, service users, carers and the public is helping integrated service provision

	OBJECTIVES					
	SERVICE IMPROVEMENT		ORGANISATIONAL IMPROVEMENTS		INVOLVEMENT PROCESS	
	STRENGTHS	WEAKNESSES	STRENGTHS	WEAKNESSES	STRENGTHS	WEAKNESSES
INDIVIDUAL SERVICE USER	• People are invited to be involved in assessment	• The assessments not well co-ordinated				
SERVICE NETWORKS			• People's views are sought on service performance across local service networks	• But they are not involved in the regular performance management of local service networks		
WHOLE SYSTEM	• Users raise issues about health economies	• No health-economy-wide forums exist in which to handle these issues			• Many measures are in place to consult people on overall strategies	• It is difficult to know whether users' views translate into service developments

are translated into practice are unclear. This makes it difficult to discern whether and how service users' views affect new service developments.

Service users often raise issues about the integration of community and acute sector services across health and social care. However, in our example, there are no mechanisms for bringing service users together across the health economies that service their local area. It is therefore impossible for service users to communicate with the acute sector providers, partnership organisations, LAs and PCTs that comprise those economies, or with service users from other areas.

> **TRY THIS**
>
> ## Improving involvement
> - Write down a list of the involvement processes your organisation uses.
> - Use what you have read in this chapter to identify the strengths and weaknesses of the engagement processes at the three levels of integration.
> - Record your results in a table similar to table 4.
> - Review your analysis and identify possible opportunities to develop the effectiveness of user involvement.

Developing an integrated approach to involving people

Your efforts to involve users, carers and members of the public will not work if you treat doing so as a separate process or as an 'add-on' to the things your organisation normally does. Nor is it as simple a matter as designing some technically effective activities. Different groups of patients, service users, carers and the public will have different and often conflicting concerns, interests or aspirations. Furthermore, these may or may not coincide with those of the service staff, managers or elected members. The picture is likely to be very complex, and both 'capital-P' and 'small-p' politics will greatly influence how a system of involving people works, and its outcomes.

At the same time as organisations are seeking integration, they still have their individual core business to take care of. There is therefore a danger that the new developments will become centred on organisations and service sectors rather than on integrated approaches to meeting the needs of patients, service users and carers.

We end this chapter with a list of the major issues concerning people's involvement that you should take into account if you seriously want to promote integration.

Checklist of ways of involving people – in health, social care and the LA more broadly – that are relevant to service integration
- **Establish basic principles**. To ensure that involving users, carers and members of the public doesn't become just a routine or an add-on, it is essential that you gain agreement amongst staff in all the services seeking integration about why this involvement is important. So you need to link it into the mainstream processes of planning, performance management and decision-making (see box 4a). Agreeing a set

of common principles across health and social care will provide a basis for ensuring effective integration.

- **Build on and develop what already exists**. Many places already have a range of ways of enabling public involvement. This might include: citizens panels, community or area forums, young people's parliaments, and reference groups for different users' needs. These may be augmented by existing advocacy, one-stop shop, call centre and advice services. The processes will have strengths and weaknesses, overlaps and gaps: these should be audited, with the help of the people they involve. Together with them, you will need to consider how to make links with the new NHS structures and processes as well as how to find the resources for the training and support needs that involvement will highlight. Table 4 (see earlier) provides a simple means of auditing your current practice.

- **Use existing knowledge**. People appreciate being consulted but they also want action. There is now a vast amount of information available about the concerns and aspirations of different groups of patients, service users and carers. Many of the issues about access and service co-ordination apply across the range of different services. Make a list of these and help others in your organisation to use it as a common health and social care 'checklist' to guide all attempts at redesigning services. This will not only make for good service development but also indicate to patients, service users and carers that you are serious about acting on what you learn through consulting people.

> ### 4a. Thurrock: Monitoring the quality of services
>
> The contracts unit in Thurrock has developed a system to ascertain users' views on the quality of the care provided by domiciliary care agencies. Each time a service user is reviewed, they are asked to complete a questionnaire about the service they are receiving. These are collated and compared to the average performance of all providers. The contracts unit then feeds back this information to the providers at their monitoring meetings.
>
> Source: *Tracking the Changes*, Joint Reviews, Audit Commission, 2002

- **Engage with the politics**. A workable system cannot be designed without taking into account both 'capital-P' and 'small-p' politics: the actions of elected members, managers and professionals as well as of different groups of users and carers (see box 4b). Any system must also be able to engage with single issue groups and to handle broader involvement. This will necessarily involve joint approaches to community development by health and LAs, reflected in common approaches to supporting community groups.

- **Be fit for purpose**. When you are thinking through your plans for an integrated approach, look for ways to deal both with the concerns of individuals and with wider, strategic issues. Whose responsibility will it be to analyse the nature of individual issues – and results of handling them – so that you can draw out the strategic lessons? In health, this fits into the role of the CPPIH local network staff, and something similar is needed in LAs to cover social care and related services. Joint reports summarising common, and linked, issues should be a regular feature of this work and should

> ### 4b. Hammersmith and Fulham: Better government for older people
>
> Regular, large events have been held for older people. An event for 80 people was held shortly after the NSF to consider the implications for the care community. Older people were keen to add a small number of additional local priorities, including transport, housing and support for carers. This is now reflected in Hammersmith and Fulham 'vision for the future'. The event also reviewed the composition of the local Whole Systems Group and, as a result, the contribution of the voluntary sector was strengthened.
> Source: *Integrated Services for Older People*, Audit Commission, October 2002

be fed back to the relevant boards and the scrutiny, clinical governance and best value processes.

- **Work with the SHAs.** With their performance management overview, SHAs are able to supply a collective view of how well PCTs, acute trusts and social care are working together. This should regularly be made available to forums of patients, service users and carers. It needs to be supplemented by face-to-face meetings with SHAs in which reports from patients and service user forums are passed to the SHA. Equally, links should be developed between user involvement and the overview and scrutiny of health. This will make it possible to scrutinise how seriously the SHA is taking users' concerns in its resource allocation and performance management processes. So it is important to ensure that scrutiny addresses the determinants of health, and health and social care integration, as well as the functioning of the NHS.

- **Make sure engagement is broad.** Don't end up relying on a small group of people to fill all the representative posts. You will risk 'burn out' and representation will suffer.

> ### 4c. Dudley and Cornwall: service user and carer representation in planning
>
> In Dudley, the main planning and implementation group (the mental health board) had two service user and two carer representatives. Service users were supported in this role by a local advocacy agency, and carers by the local carers development workers. They would hold briefings prior to the board meetings.
>
> In Cornwall, mental health user forums had been in place for some years. They were supported by a user forum co-ordinator employed by the local rural community council. Similar arrangements existed for carers who were supported by the county carers' co-ordinator. Both were members of the local NSF Implementation Team.
>
> Source: *Modernising Mental Health Services*, Social Services Inspectorate, DoH, June 2002

Representation is not just about having people on committees and forums. You also have to develop outreach work, and put resources into it: literally reach out to people – especially those from socially excluded groups – who would not otherwise put themselves forward as representatives. When people do put themselves forward, how will you make sure they get the support they need to be able to operate effectively? (See box 4c.) It is unlikely that any single organisation will be able to afford the continuing investment this requires, so pooling your involvement budgets and sharing common infrastructure, such as citizens panels, becomes an attractive option.

TRY THIS

Using engagement to support integration

Our checklist refers to the set of health, social care and broader LA involvement processes that are relevant to service integration. Check that, as a set, these support integration:

To promote an integrated approach:
- Establish basic principles
- Build on and develop what exists
- Use existing knowledge
- Engage with the politics
- Be fit for purpose
- Work with the SHAs
- Make sure engagement is broad.

- Apply the checklist to your own organisation's arrangements and assess their strengths and weaknesses.
- Identify the changes that will be required in:
  - overall partnership strategies
  - core business plans
  - involvement processes
- Allocate responsibility for ensuring that there is progress on these changes, and decide appropriate monitoring arrangements.

Chapter five: Financing

When two or more organisations consider integrating their services, they are accepting the possibility of allocating their resources in a more co-ordinated way to achieve common objectives. These objectives will relate to improved services but may also include an intention to reduce the overhead costs of managing their budgets.

In most cases, organisations will not be considering a merger of all their services, which could be seen as the ultimate integration. Most will want to develop ways to align or pool a proportion of their resources whilst maintaining their status as distinct organisations. This has implications, including the following.

- Allocating a proportion of total resources in this way may have an impact on how the remainder is managed.
- Negotiations about integration are most likely to be successful if each organisation understands the constraints within which the other organisations have to manage their total resources.
- Each organisation will need to maintain effective financial accountability. They need to be convinced that all partners are committed to any joint arrangement and that each is sufficiently competent in managing its overall budgets so as to be sure that the pooled budget is not put at risk.

Local government finance

The majority of local government funding comes from the Revenue Support Grant provided by central government. The other main sources are local council tax and income from charges. The total amount an LA can spend each year is capped by central government and is linked to formulae about needs in the local population called the Standard Spending Assessment (SSA). Once an LA knows what its cap is and how much funding it will receive from central government, it sets council tax rates to bring its funding to a level up to or below the cap.

Most funding is open to be spent on the services that each council decides are a priority. The overall SSA is broken down into sub-totals suggesting how much should be spent in broad areas of service such as education and social care, but a council can decide to spend above or below SSA in any service. Expenditure above SSA in one service might therefore lead to a less-than-SSA level in another.

However some funding is 'ring-fenced', that is, only to be used only for certain services. If an LA provides housing, for instance, the costs associated with this must be met from income from rents. The Housing Revenue Account (HRA) (which comprises incomes from rents) cannot be used for non-housing services; this also applies to housing associations set up to manage council housing. The LA will have a small budget outside the HRA to use on strategic housing responsibilities such as influencing the overall rented market and liaising with registered social landlords.

In education, LAs must devolve 85 per cent of expenditure to schools (School Standards and Framework Act, 1998), which can then choose how this money is used. The rest is held by the LA to meet specialist education needs and to ensure the overall strategic planning of services, including partnerships with other organisations to cover activities such as regeneration, child protection and welfare.

LAs also receive ring-fenced special grants attached to policy initiatives. Examples include funds to help reduce delayed hospital discharges, or for training or for developing mental health services.

LAs are large purchasers of services from external providers in areas like social care, environmental services, IT and telecommunications and much of this is linked to annual, legally enforceable contracts. They also give grants to voluntary organisations that are seen as providing valuable community-based services.

Councillors are legally responsible for agreeing a budget that stays within the spending limits set, and can be individually surcharged if they fail to do so.

NHS finance

In the NHS, primary care trusts (PCTs) have responsibility for commissioning and providing health care for their local population. This includes acute, community and primary care services. Some specialist services may be commissioned by the SHA. PCTs have to bid for their funds each year within a national 'service and financial framework'.

Local government income from charges

As we described above, an LA will receive part of its income from charges. There are three types of charges.

- Some charges are mandatory and fixed, such as those linked to the issuing of various licences. None of these relate to social care.
- Some are mandatory but not fixed, such as those for residential and nursing home places, where national means testing rules apply but local decisions are made about charges. The level of charges is linked to the costs of providing or purchasing places.

- Some are discretionary and not fixed, such as those for home care, day care and respite care. Most authorities decide to charge for these services because central government funding levels are based on an assumption that income will be raised through such charges. They are usually progressive and linked to means testing and the quantity of a service being provided.

The services that are most likely to be subject to pooled budgets – community based support including home care, occupational therapy, intermediate care, etc. – fit into the third category, where charges are discretionary. The law is clear that NHS services must be free at the point of delivery and, with the exception of things like dental care and prescriptions, health services are not charged for. Therefore a person receiving a combination of 'health' and 'social' care services could only be charged for the social care portion.

The value of pooled budgets, as described earlier, is that there is no need to label some needs as 'social' or 'health' since the expenditure doesn't have to be recorded in this way. This flexibility allows front-line staff to provide flexible, tailor-made packages of care, the components of which can be changed as needs change. However if charges are to be applied for the 'non-health' element of care, then staff have to revert to the previous, more inflexible approach of defining the proportions of a care package that are social care. As the law stands, the challenge for health and social care organisations is to move towards more integrated budgetary arrangements without social services losing large amounts of income and whilst staying within the law.

The national guidance on intermediate care services is that they should be provided free. Where intermediate care is only provided for up to six weeks, this involves less loss of income for social services than would be the case if a similar approach were taken to longer term care. In some areas, arrangements have been agreed for PCTs to contribute funds to social services to compensate for the loss of income that results from providing intermediate care services free of charge. The challenges of charging may be one reason for deciding to have aligned rather than pooled budgets.

It is important to provide information on charges to individual service users when they are considering what services are best for them. If charges are to be levied, there

---

TRY THIS

Integrating budgetary systems

When people talk about health and social care budgetary systems, they usually highlight the differences. However, if integration is to work, we need to capitalise on the similarities and manage the differences.

Assess what needs to be done locally by:
- Similarities – listing the fundamental similarities between the health and social care budgetary systems and how they can be harnessed locally to enable integration.
- Differences – describing the main differences and what can be done to manage them in such a way as to maintain the greatest degree of integration.

must be a clear system for explaining them. Where services are integrated, the link worker for a combined package of care may be an NHS employee. For NHS staff, the practice of charging and assessing individual means will be new and represent a change of ideology. These staff need clear procedures and training to enable them to explain, and in some cases implement, any charging policies and ensure that information to users is consistent.

Pooled budgets and aligned budgets

As with other aspects of integration there are ways of increasing integration that do not involve the Health Act flexibilities. Pooled budgets – which we described in chapter one – involve transferring funds into a joint pool that can be used flexibly to meet needs. A partnership agreement to set up a pooled budget will require the partners to agree:

- how much each partner will contribute
- what level of budget variation, both in and between years, will be acceptable to partners
- how inflation will be managed
- nature, timing and financial management information and arrangements
- details of the partnership service delivery contracts
- LA charging policies.

Aligning budgets means two or more organisations identifying specific sums of money that they will use in a complementary way to achieve a common outcome.

Because aligned budgets are not defined in the law or policy, choices can be made about how they are set up and managed. The issues that require clarification include the following.

- For what purpose are the budgets being used? Is there a single set of objectives?

> **TRY THIS**
>
> ## Getting the best out of aligned and pooled budgets
>
> Aligned and pooled budgets are often wrongly discussed as if they are competing alternatives. In practice they are options to be drawn on to support integration depending on the local conditions.
> - Draw up a list of conditions under which aligned budgets would best suit your local needs, and those under which pooled budgets would be preferable.

- How much money is involved and over what time period?
- What are the expectations about volume and type of service coming from this resource?
- Who will control each budget?
- How and what information will be shared between budget holders about actual and projected expenditure and any risk factors?
- How will expenditure be matched to outcomes?

Devolving expenditure to front-line staff

A major benefit of pooled budgets is the potential to use funds to meet individual needs without having to define those needs as either 'health' or 'social'. The policy also allows staff from health or local government to be holders of a pooled budget. In addition to a single overall budget manager, organisations can identify a number of staff closer to the front line who will manage a portion of the total budget.

Organisations contributing to the pool need to know that the money is being spent in line with their own overall objectives. So they need to agree about a number of things, including:

- the formula for deciding the size of the budget a person will control. Should it be based on the patterns of need in the population, the way money has been spent in the past, or what?
- any rules about spreading spending over time so that money doesn't run out before the end of the year.
- systems for record keeping and monitoring spending. If part of a pool is represented by directly employed staff, then ways of accounting for their time must be agreed.
- rules about funding the care of people with very high level individual needs that require unusually expensive or long-term care.

For staff in social services, this may mean having care managers in control of budgets that were previously held by their own managers. These people will, however, be familiar with the notion of a purchasing budget. In the NHS, by contrast, it is very rare for front-line staff to control cash budgets for purchasing care: expenditure takes place through the allocation of staff time. An integrated approach means all budget holders will be working to the same procedures.

Risk management

One of the advantages of having a large overall budget is the potential it gives to spread risk. If budget rules allow it, it's possible to offset overspending in one area with underspending in another. A large overall budget also provides greater capacity to respond to unanticipated demands for expenditure. Risk management of this type takes place in both local government and the NHS. Within social services, funds may be transferred between budgets: between, for example, services for adults and services for children. Equally, if the total LA budget is in difficulty, any budgets that are not ring-fenced may be called on to cover a deficit elsewhere.

In the NHS, PCTs are now responsible for the allocation of resources into each local health economy. As was the case with health authorities in the past, the PCTs may face pressure to transfer funds in order to cover extra costs such as new prescribing guidance from the National Institute for Clinical Excellence (NICE) or to meet growing pressure on accident and emergency services. But where health authorities played a brokerage role in responding to under- or overspending within their areas, the PCTs have less scope to do this because their budgets are smaller. There is, however, already some evidence of SHAs expecting PCTs in a better financial position to bail out PCTs that are having problems.

The larger the proportion of a budget that is identified for integration of some sort, the greater the need for early discussion between partner organisations about approaches to risk management. For example, were a pooled budget to be established, could one party withdraw funds to meet an emergency?

The other aspect of risk management is the impact that pooling some budgets can have on other budgets that remain within single organisational control. In local government, a decision to pool a substantial part of the older people's budgets may reduce the ability to balance the budgets within social services.

Integrated financial systems will operate within a wider context of overall financial management. Organisations entering into new arrangements will need to consider how competently their partners will control risks to their finances. For example, a poor report from the Audit Commission (local government) or the Commission for Health Improvement (health) might indicate potential problems, even if the managers in the integrated services are competent.

Partner organisations contemplating pooling budgets need systematically and realistically to assess each organisation's status as a potential contributor to and/or manager of a pooled budget. Table 5.1 shows the main factors to consider, set out against each of the three levels of integration, with some examples of questions to ask.

table 5.1 Some examples of the horizontal integration of commissioning			
	ADEQUACY OF EXISTING RESOURCE LEVELS	EVIDENCE OF EFFECTIVE FINANCIAL MANAGEMENT	THE IMPACT OF WIDER FINANCIAL SYSTEMS ON BUDGETARY CONTROL
INDIVIDUAL SERVICE USER	• What is the position regarding waiting lists for services?	• Does the organisation have systems for monitoring expenditure related to individual service users?	• Is the balance between crisis intervention and prevention correct and financially sustainable?
SERVICE NETWORKS	• What is the position regarding vacancies, turnover and use of agency staff?	• What systems exist for monitoring delegated budgets?	• Do budget allocations take into account differences in needs between localities?
WHOLE SYSTEM	• What is the budget position, over- or underspending?	• Are budget and performance management integrated and focused on outcomes?	• What service areas are in competition for resources and are they high risk?

Accounting for overheads

Many budgets held within a large organisation will contain an element to reflect the contribution of corporate support services to the running of a particular service. These can include accommodation costs, human resources support, IT and communications. Sometimes these elements are fully under the control of the particular budget holder who has a choice about what and how much of these overheads to purchase. More often the budget holder has no option but to use the corporate services and cannot spend the budget on an alternative. There are three issues to consider.

- How do you ensure that increases or decreases in corporate overheads are re-allocated fairly? For example, if a substantial budget is put into a pool, how will the overheads previously met from within the budget be covered?
- If a new hybrid service is being set up with a pooled budget, how will the service receive necessary infrastructure support and how will this be funded?
- If the new service is allowed to choose an alternative supplier of support, what impact might that have on other services that may have to bear a larger proportion of the cost of overheads?

Budget management

At a corporate level, organisations need to consider the overall effect of establishing financial integration in various service areas. It is possible to have a variety of arrangements that present different challenges from the management of traditional budgets. If organisations decide not to go down the route of total integration in the form of a care trust, then they are more likely to develop numerous partnership arrangements. All financial arrangements will require support in the form of financial expertise, auditing and monitoring systems. As the variety of arrangements develop, you will need to think about how this support will be provided and to what extent it should be centralised or devolved.

TRY THIS

Managing a system of pooled and aligned budgets

Much of the discussion about aligned and pooled budgets is centred on the management of individual budgets. However the ability to sustain these budget arrangements, and their overall success, depends on how the entire system of separate, aligned and pooled budgets is managed.

Thinking about your own system,
- try to outline the full extent to which budgets will need to be aligned and pooled to support integration.
- What similarities and differences will there be in moving control of these budgets to front-line staff? Are these going to be manageable?
- Should the way overheads are allocated to the different aligned and pooled budgets be the same or should they vary?
- Will the way that overspending and underspending are currently treated (across health and social care) have to change to keep the aligned and pooled budgets appropriately under control?
- What are the corporate implications likely to be?

Chapter six: Human resource management

People are an integrated service's major resource. Good human resource management (HRM) will make a crucial difference to its ability to keep and develop skilled, motivated staff. Integration has implications for HRM when: a) the new organisation is being designed; b) resources and other support have to be found for HRM; and c) the transition into the new, integrated organisation is under way.

a) Designing the new organisation

The integration of services usually happens in stages. At the beginning, you cannot simply sit down and draft a detailed, final structure and set of working arrangements; these will need to be shaped and re-shaped as the integrated organisation evolves. What you *can* do, however, is describe the overall pattern of working and the main changes in roles and teams that will be needed to secure the first stage of integration. This process can then be repeated as services integrate further.

Overall impact

The first step is to get an overview of the set of proposed changes and the impact they are likely to have on staff at the three levels of integration (see table 6.1 which uses the introduction of an intermediate care scheme as an example).

This example shows the proposed integration will affect more than the staff in the scheme itself. The work undertaken by teams working 'upstream' and 'downstream'

table 6.1: The overall impact of proposed integration. Example: intermediate care	
INDIVIDUAL SERVICE USER	LIKELY IMPACT • Intensive, time limited work by an integrated team
SERVICE NETWORKS	• Changes some of the work previously undertaken by the teams 'upstream' and 'downstream' from the intermediate care scheme
WHOLE SYSTEM	• Puts pressure on the need for an integrated assessment process and the integrated management of care pathways. Will change the demand for, and use of, acute and independent sector providers of home and residential care

from the care scheme will also change. For example, the scheme will take over some of their previous co-ordination roles. The intended impact of the scheme is to enable more people to live at home, independently or with support. This will change the pattern of demand and the work of the acute, home care and residential care sectors. For example, rehabilitation previously undertaken in the acute sector will now take place through the scheme, which may contract with some residential care providers. Finally, intermediate care schemes are moving towards adopting integrated assessment. This is likely to put pressure on the whole service system to come into line.

The impact on roles and teams

The initial overall analysis will help you identify the major impacts on the service system. Now you need to undertake a more detailed analysis to 'unpack' the likely impact on particular teams and individual staff roles.

Roles: Often integration requires a different range of roles, with different responsibilities and skill mixes from those currently found in the individual services (see box 6a). This does not imply that you need a wholesale change in people's roles but, rather, a reassessment of the profile of jobs. This 'reprofiling' will comprise a combination of three types of change:

- the creation of some completely new roles, for example, generic workers who combine activities previously done by people in separate posts, such as staff who undertake core assessments in health and social care.

> ### TRY THIS
>
> ## Identifying the impact of a set of service integrations
>
> Usually several service integrations are being planned at the same time, all of which may have implications for the work undertaken by the same sets of staff. To check whether this is so, and the cumulative effects of these changes:
> - List the planned service integrations, for example, integrated assessments, intermediate care, a customer contact centre.
> - For each innovation use table 6.1 to identify the likely impacts.
> - Analyse your cumulative results to identify which groups of staff will be affected in what ways.

- the extension and development of existing roles, for example, enabling nurses to prescribe and home care workers to take on some nursing tasks.
- new integrated working practices. In many roles, the tasks to be undertaken will remain unchanged but the way in which some of them – such as assessment – are to be carried out will change. The range of patients, service users and carers with whom these staff work may also change.

Teams: Integration will alter the make up and boundaries of many of the teams in which staff currently work. This may include changes such as:
- the creation of completely new teams – as has happened in intermediate care

- the merger of existing teams – a familiar occurrence in the creation of community mental health and learning disabilities teams
- linked teams – where existing team boundaries are retained but specific teams are required to work together using joint protocols to provide the integrated service. This may also involve co-location or the designation of link workers, for example, attaching specific social workers from a team to particular GP practices.

What will the new integrated service look like?

Teams and roles

To get a clearer idea of the shape of the evolving integrated service, you can break it down into its component parts and 'map' the changes that will be required in roles and teams for it to be effective. Table 6.2 uses the distinctions we made earlier between different degrees of change in roles and teams to provide an example of what might stay the same and what might change, and how.

The example in the table, of the development of an intermediate care team in a particular locality, shows how roles and teams need to change both in the intermediate care team itself and in other teams that link with it.

- Some new generic worker posts will be created. An integrated assessment and care planning process will be established, affecting both the new generic worker posts and those of the community nurses and social workers in the new team. The community nurses and social workers will share some defined tasks.
- Each intermediate care team will be linked to a specific set of community nursing and social work teams. All teams will use the same integrated assessment and care planning process. Existing separate community nursing and social work teams will be retained: they will refer to, and follow on from, the work of the intermediate care team.

In this example, only the staff joining the new intermediate care team are required to change teams. They will experience the biggest changes, both joining a new team and

---

6a. North Derbyshire: changing roles

As a pilot site within the NHS Changing Workforce Programme, North Derbyshire is looking at new ways of working in relation to care of older people across NHS and social care. The pilot aims to develop, test and implement changing roles for health and social care staff that will support the delivery of patient care and the NSF. Objectives include providing continuity of care throughout the 'patient journey' and reducing the number of unnecessary handovers and reassessments. The North Derbyshire pilot brings together several strands, two of which aim to provide home care staff with new skills in rehabilitation and in supervising medication. Although it is its early stages, the pilot is already demonstrating promising results. In some cases, for example, training a home help to administer eye drops has reduced by half the number of daily visits that older people need.

Source: *Integrated Services for Older People*, Audit Commission, October 2002

table 6.2 What changes will need to be made in roles and teams? Example: intermediate care			
	NEW ROLES	EXTENDED ROLES	EXISTING ROLES BUT INTEGRATED PRACTICE
NEW TEAMS	• Intermediate care team – new generic worker roles	• Intermediate care team – community nurses and social workers share some tasks and use integrated assessment and care planning processes	
MERGED TEAMS			
LINKED TEAMS			• Existing community nursing and social work teams – linked to specific intermediate care teams and use integrated assessment and care planning process

taking on completely new or extended roles. But the table helps us to see that, were we to consider only changes in intermediate care, we would gain the false impression that staff in other teams will not experience much change. In fact, all staff will have to take on new ways of working. They will be using the integrated assessment and care planning process, linking with new sets of teams and forging new working relationships.

Changes in working conditions

Although they are both working in the public service, NHS and LA social care have developed very different terms of employment and working conditions for their staff. Bringing staff from different sectors into integrated teams will sooner or later raise staff awareness of any differences in pay

TRY THIS

Detailed service integration design

New service integrations will require changes in existing working relationships and the establishment of new ones. You can identify the details of who is affected, and how, by:

- choosing one of your planned service integrations
- identifying the roles and teams that will:
  — be changed
  — have to work differently
  — experience a change in demand for their services
- logging the likely impacts on each of the roles and teams affected, using table 6.2
- developing a process for engaging those affected in the detailed design and implementation process.

scales, leave entitlement and other benefits. Where the differences are small, they may pose few problems. But larger differences may prove more difficult to handle. For example, LA moves to abolish the differences in terms and conditions between blue and white collar jobs – known as 'single status' – may appear at odds with terms and conditions for health service staff where that distinction remains.

If you are aiming to improve outcomes for the public, your integrated service will have to be there at the times people most need it. So many services will have to offer extended opening hours or be open at weekends or even on a 24 hour basis. This could mean introducing permanent shift systems, various forms of cover arrangements and part-time working. The impact of this flexible working will be uneven, affecting only some groups of staff. Those who have been employed on a nominal 9 to 5, five day working week are likely to feel the change more acutely than those who have always worked shifts. Some will not wish to change; others may welcome the flexible hours as a way of achieving a better work life balance. What is important is to treat people as individuals whose needs will differ and to take that into account when introducing change.

People who have opted to work in integrated pilot projects are often prepared to live with differences in terms and conditions to be part of a boundary-breaking innovation. However, as pilots turn into mainstream services, the reality of these differences may become more important and need tackling.

However, it is important not to assume that differences in terms and conditions will necessarily cause problems. Sometimes, differences can, in effect, cancel each other out; at other times, the differences are so small, they are of little concern to staff. The most important thing in handling potential differences is to make sure that all staff are aware of the terms and conditions that apply to all the posts within their teams. This will both clarify the position and also scotch any myths that can otherwise quickly build up about inequality. Table 6.3 lists the key points to cover.

> **TUPE or not?**
> Issues about terms and conditions typically arise in three situations. The first is 'outposting', where staff are employed, managed and paid by their existing employer, but are located in another organisation. The second is secondment, where staff are employed and paid by their existing employer but are located in and managed by another organisation. TUPE – where the move involves a legal 'transfer of undertaking' – is the third situation, but not always an easy one to define. Whether a 'transfer of undertaking' is occurring is a matter of interpretation (see the box) and is likely to be affected by the continuing development of case law. Outposting and secondment both involve the alignment of terms and conditions between the two employing organisations. Under TUPE, however, it is the new employing organisation that will have to handle any changes.
>
> The main differences of legal interpretation revolve around whether the TUPE requirement is triggered by the transfer of staff to the operational control of the new organisation or whether it also requires the transfer of responsibility for securing services. If the former interpretation is used, then all moves to partnership or care trusts will trigger TUPE. If the latter interpretation is used then, as long as each sector is held responsible for securing its own outcomes via the integrated organisation, secondment is an option.

Staff development and training

All staff, not just those taking on new and extended roles, will need training and continuing development to be able to function effectively in the new integrated service (see box 6b). This staff development and training may need to cover:

- **the changing environment** – national and local imperatives that are driving forward integration, as well as how health and social care services are currently organised and the planned changes.
- **the ideology of integrated practice** – adopting the responsibility for ensuring improved outcomes for people; the philosophy behind integration; and relationships with service users, carers and patients, other staff and the general public
- the introduction of new, more effective, **evidence-based practices**.
- **integrated working practices** – collaborating with other staff, using new systems and protocols, including tasks not previously undertaken by different groups of staff.

Most staff development occurs on the job, using everyday working practices such as supervision and team meetings; through the performance management and appraisal mechanisms; and through developments such as clinical governance, best value and quality assurance. It is essential, therefore, to find ways of building learning into all these activities. You will want to ensure, for instance, that the routine means by which work and performance are assessed, allocated, supported and managed are oriented towards

---

table 6.3: Important terms and conditions

- Pay scales, overtime, bonuses and enhancements
- Annual leave and time off in lieu
- Expected working hours and work – life balance
- Maternity, paternity, dependency and sick leave
- Employer and employer pensions contributions and benefits
- Car purchase, leasing, mileage allowances and other travel benefits
- Health and safety, including dealing with violence
- Equal opportunities and positive diversity
- Appraisal, access to training and maintenance of professional registration
- Disciplinaries, grievances and redundancy

TRY THIS

Terms and conditions

Where new teams are to be formed with cross-sector mixes of staff, bring together the human resource management staff, managers, staff and trades union representatives to:
- produce an analysis of the similarities and differences on terms and conditions
- list those which will have to change to:
  —fit the new service
  — ensure equity between staff
- identify those changes which:
  — can be negotiated locally
  – require national agreement
- develop an action plan.

promoting integration. This applies as much to individual teams as it does to strategic management and partnerships. Here are some practical examples. Establish routine meetings across local service networks and ensure these allow time for analysis and joint problem solving. Use the processes of best value, clinical governance and quality assurance to focus people's attention on the way they are providing an integrated service.

> ## 6b. Northumberland: Integrated teams
>
> In Northumberland, four rehabilitation teams operate within the care trust. These are integrated health and social care teams, which are made up of a co-ordinator from either an NHS or social services background, occupational therapy and generic rehabilitation workers and dedicated physiotherapy and speech and language therapy input. The generic staff have an intensive induction programme and a foundation course on stroke and are expected to pass NVQ Level 3 (Promoting Independence)
>
> Source: *Integrated Services for Older People*, Audit Commission, October 2002

Make structured use of on the job training, staff exchanges, placements and shadowing. Set up events such as workshops, 'action learning networks'(where people meet regularly to focus on an aspect of their work and share their combined experience), away-days, conferences and qualifying courses.

Local staff development and training must be the main priority in enabling staff to get the best out of service integration. However it is essential that local training and development is matched by changes in the qualifications frameworks and training provided nationally in health and social care. The ability to work in integrated service systems, and training for extended or integrated roles, are now on the national training agenda. Trials are under way of some new developments, such as common foundation years for health and social care trainees and practice placements in others sectors or integrated settings. But sector-focused views of training still predominate and this will have to be addressed.

There is room for this. In health, many of the professions are legally self-regulating and set the standards required to become a member and retain membership. But, in both health and social care, training providers have much leeway, outside of core requirements, to vary the content and methods within qualifying courses. Employer and employee bodies – the workforce confederations in health and TOPSS, which is the sector skills council for social care – seek to

> ## TRY THIS
>
> ## Identifying the training and staff development implications of integration
>
> Use the examples we have given of potential staff development and training needs to identify:
> - which groups of staff will require what staff development and training
> - how development and training for existing staff should be designed and run
> - what the implications are for qualifying training and how to negotiate appropriate changes.

influence training and, in large areas of health, they directly commission much of the professional training. The role of the employer–employee bodies is even stronger in determining the training for staff not in the established professions, particularly through the content of NVQ qualifications. As these staff make up a very large proportion of the total workforce, this provides a big opportunity to directly affect training for integration.

Changes, both locally and nationally, are bound to have an impact on staff's perception of both their jobs and what now constitute career options. Career paths that involve more integrated working and moves into and out of new generic roles will become the norm. The opportunities and advantages of such career paths need to be made clear when advertising vacancies. Existing requirements for professional practice maintenance and development may need to be adapted to enable staff to retain flexible career options.

b) Resourcing and supporting HRM

Much of the HRM work in both health and social care – for example, staff recruitment and selection – is done by operational managers, but they are often supported by HRM sections. These sections may be located within the relevant NHS or social care organisation, or they may be located more centrally within an LA or in an NHS shared services organisation, or they may be outsourced to a private sector provider of LA corporate and departmental support services. NHS shared services organisations are typically located within an existing trust which takes on the functions on behalf of other local trusts.

Integration is likely to require changes in these support arrangements to enable a number of important questions to be tackled:

- **the development and interpretation of employment policy**. Who works out the local implications of changes in European and UK national entities employment and case law, national agreements and changes in professional self regulation?
- **the development of local employment policy**. Will NHS bodies, with shared HRM services, be adopting shared local employment policies and how will LA-wide policies be applied to partnership bodies or seconded employees? What arrangements should there be for working and negotiating locally with trade unions?
- **HRM 'processing functions'**. Who will provide the infrastructure and staff to ensure that essential HRM processing functions – such as recruitment and staff selection and police checks; performance management and appraisals, training and career development; maintenance of staff records; negotiation of local pay deals; and disciplinary and grievance procedures – run smoothly?
- **operational management**. Regardless of the final employing authority, what HRM decisions should be delegated to front-line and other operational managers? What

generic practices should be agreed so that managers do not use different approaches to the same HRM task, such as appraisal, depending on who employs which member of their staff

In the initial stages of service integration, it may be possible to support the needs of both the new integrated service and any new partnership organisation by keeping existing HRM staff in their current locations. But you will have to think about whether this may need to change in the future. This is likely to involve a choice between two locations:

- **partnership organisations**. HRM staff for whom there is a high volume of work, and with whom close liaison is required, may be relocated to the partnership organisation.

- **shared servicing**. Matters which are the same across sectors (such as the interpretation of employment law) or shared within a sector (for example, job grading) or too expensive for the partnership organisation to provide its own, may be handled by a shared services agency. This might be one of the local partnership or care trusts, an existing NHS shared services provider, an LA-wide corporate service, or an independent private sector provider.

The choice will partly be a pragmatic one. You will want, for example, to minimise disruption, take into account the various needs of the integrated organisation and be able to handle the knock-on effects that will arise if you 'unbundle' the HRM services from their existing location. So it is essential to be clear both what the current arrangements are and what arrangements are required in their place. You can use table 6.4 (overleaf) to help you build a picture of your current arrangements.

Deciding whether or not to use shared servicing, and what for, raises a number of issues. Arguments in favour of a move towards shared servicing are:

- **harmonised terms and conditions**. Having shared HRM expertise in one place makes it easier to identify and negotiate changes in locally-determined terms and conditions and feed these into national negotiations.

- **affordability**. In some areas, services may be integrated through a range of partnership bodies. Many of these may be too small to afford HRM support functions of their own.

- **efficiency**. Many HRM support tasks are generic and could be more efficiently done by a single HRM provider.

- **the promotion of synergy**. Spotting common trends across the workforce, commissioning integrated training from training providers and promoting new career paths all require a cross-sector approach to HRM.

- **symbolic significance**. Changing the way something is organised can, in itself, be a way of symbolising and giving legitimacy to your willingness to revise any or all of the current HRM practices in support of integration.

table 6.4: Human resource management – who, does what and where?						
	LINE MANAGERS IN AN NHS, SOCIAL CARE OR PARTNERSHIP ORGANISATION		HRM LOCATED IN AN NHS, SOCIAL CARE OR PARTNERSHIP ORGANISATION		CORPORATE LA, NHS SHARED SERVICES OR OUTSOURCED	
	HEALTH	SOCIAL CARE	HEALTH	SOCIAL CARE	HEALTH	SOCIAL CARE
Developing and interpreting national and European employment policy						
Developing local employment policy						
Recruitment and staff selection						
Pay and conditions						
Performance management and appraisals						
Training and staff development						
Disciplinary and grievance procedures						
Equal opportunities and positive diversity						
Health and safety						
Industrial relations						

The arguments for keeping part or all of HRM within existing health or social care organisations or in new partnership bodies are:

- **minimum disruption**. Retaining as many viable parts of HRM as possible in their current organisations helps to maintain continuity.
- **retention of identity**. Where there are concerns over who should ultimately govern integrated services, keeping at least some HRM in separate health and social care organisations can be seen as reinforcing the different governance positions.

TRY THIS

Redesigning HRM support for integration

There will often be a number of options for providing HRM support to enable integration. You can identify these by:
- using table 6.4 to describe who, located where, carries out which HRM work
- using the arguments we have laid out for locating HRM to identify what might be best provided by whom, in what location.

Finally, it is important not to confuse the employer of HRM staff with the locations from which they work. For example, staff working in outsourced private sector service providers on behalf of LAs are for the most part located within the appropriate departments of the LA. Bear in mind that the closer HRM people are to the staff they are supporting, the more they will be in touch with their needs and be able to provide a more customer-focused service. Also, some areas of HRM are of high enough volume or so 'mission critical' that they should be supplied within the customer's organisation.

c) Enabling the transition

The point of integration is to make existing services more effective. But you won't improve services – at least in the short term – if you lose your trained and skilled staff along the way, either literally or by not retaining their full commitment and enabling their skills to be deployed in the most effective way. They have to understand and be behind the integration; and, in respect of terms, conditions and place of employment, they have to feel secure enough to make the move. Don't expect this commitment and security to develop overnight.

A first step is to engage staff, before the integration, in planning and developing the integrated service. Make every effort to see that they 'own' the proposed changes. They will be concerned about what will happen to them, what job they will be doing, in which sort of team, and located where, and all these valid questions need answers.

But the issue that both motivates people and has the greatest power to make integration a success is their commitment to produce improved outcomes for patients, service users and carers through high quality, integrated services. So involving staff in the process of developing a service not only makes good sense in tapping their practice expertise but also as a way of developing commitment and motivation for change.

Although they are engaged in the same fundamental processes of prevention, treatment, rehabilitation and the promotion of independence, both the meanings of these words and the practices that result in them can vary, often radically, between health and social care. Time spent on enabling staff to understand differences in language, policy drivers, activities and working practices is time well spent. It provides a bedrock of understanding from which to develop the shared language and practice of integration.

Many staff have little contact with all of the services within their own sector on a day-to-day basis. Front-line staff, in particular, have only a sketchy idea of how their sectors are funded and managed. This lack of working knowledge is even greater when applied to services in other sectors. These knowledge gaps must be filled to enable all staff, patients, service users and carers to participate effectively in service development. Briefings and events such as 'information market days' are a useful way of enabling staff to understand what currently exists and what new developments are already under way.

Most of the detailed development will have to be undertaken by the staff running the services, along with patients, service users and carers. However they will need clear, solid backing from elected and board members and senior management to feel certain it is worthwhile committing time and effort to the development process. Staff will also want a 'steer' to understand in which direction they should be seeking developments and to use as a lever to persuade colleagues about the direction of change.

Good leadership allows staff the opportunity to feed back new ideas and affect the development of services as implementation proceeds. Be clear about the integrated decision making processes and ensure that people always have an up-to-date timetable for change.

Integration will always be a direction of travel rather than a destination. Services do not change overnight and new integrated organisations take time to bed down. So there will always be a need for continuing joint training. This starts with induction, but all staff need opportunities to understand the roles others perform in their own and linked teams. Shadowing and similar activities are efficient ways of developing this knowledge and, at the same time, building the new working relationships.

Keeping up to date with new developments as integration progresses will be a continuing challenge. Regular network meetings between teams that work closely together and joint training days will help. Training is also a useful way of injecting an external challenge into both the service and the process of developing the organisation. Ensure, too, that staff keep pace with emerging research evidence, guidelines from NICE and the

---

6c. Integrated team working

Basic principles

- Integrated outcomes – agreed and owned, common outcomes to be produced for patients, service users and carers
- Single systems – used by all team members for screening referrals, prioritising, assessment, care planning, recording, linking to others' services, review and workload management.
- One team meeting – attended by all staff with a common agenda
- Integrated working – collaborative action across staff groups within the team; trust in one another's judgements
- Self evaluation – regular cross-team scrutiny of practice, effective action planning and implementation.

Source: OPM

6d. St Mary's Hospital Paddington: Discharge planning

Discharge planning at St Mary's has made a demonstrable impact on delayed transfers, reducing levels of delay from about 50 or 60 per week to about 10 or 15. Very few delays now relate to older people. They have adopted an integrated team approach, empowering ward staff and changing culture, particularly among clinicians.

Source: *Integrated Services for Older People*, Audit Commission, October 2002

Social Care Institute for Excellence (SCIE) and the findings of national and local inspections.

The day-to-day working process not only maintains people's current practice but can also be a powerful medium through which to promote continuing change. This can be achieved by building ways of learning into the integrated organisation itself. We return to our three levels of integration: individual service user, service networks and the whole system.

- At the **individual service user** level, putting staff in different roles, into an integrated team, with a single manager does not guarantee integration. There are many examples of such teams where the different staff groups operate as teams within teams or as virtually independent practitioners. Neither will produce the benefits expected of integration. When forming integrated teams it is essential to spell out the key principles of integrated team working (see box 6c) and provide staff with the opportunity to understand them. These principles are so central to success that they should be incorporated into clinical governance and team self-audits and also into the formal performance management of teams.

- Integration is as much about working in integrated **service networks** as it is about working in integrated teams. Integration works best when teams are clear about which other teams they should work with, have clear rules of engagement and service standards and manage themselves as a network rather than as separate teams. Formalising service delivery networks and establishing the processes of network management not only helps to sort out day-to-day working problems but also provides a continuing mechanism for exchanging ideas and examples of good practice.

- Finally, at the **whole system** level, integrated teams and network management are part of the wider process of integrated management to provide the resources for and otherwise support the new front-line

---

6e. Portsmouth: Developing a culture of collaboration

In Portsmouth, the SSD and PCT had, over time, developed a joint approach between four or five key players who had worked in the area, in different roles. All shared a practical, problem solving focus. If funds were available, they would test out new ways of working, often based on experience from elsewhere. All the partner agencies tended to consider each other's needs and would take a flexible approach to considering what might be achieved and now to improve services for older people with the resources they had jointly available.

Source: *Integrated Services for Older People*, Audit Commission, October 2002

TRY THIS

Check your implementation plan

Read through what we have outlined as the elements that enable staff to 'own' the move to greater integration to decide how best to engage staff in:
- developing the implementation plan
- putting the plan into action.

practice. Whatever form it takes, managers will need opportunities to understand the organisational processes and structures that currently exist in health and social care and those developing in any new integrated organisations, where they exist. You will also have to work on bringing together the different 'drivers' on health and social care so that operational managers can understand them, make best use of the synergies between them and find ways of managing the conflicts. Overall, it is a flexible culture of collaboration (see box 6e) that needs to be developed.

Chapter seven: Information and ICT

People sometimes believe that the best way to provide integrated information is by developing an information and communication technology (ICT) based system. It is not.

Before information can be shared, people have to agree what information is needed to support which activities. They must trust that the information will be kept secure and not be misused. They must understand and value one another's skills enough to feel confident in acting on information that others have collected. Managers must be able to demonstrate that the structured use of information does inform their planning and decision making. Cracking the information sharing problem is thus as much to do with cultural and organisational change and information management as it is to do with ICT. The main questions to be asked are:

a)   Why is better and more integrated information needed?

b)   What information is needed?

c)   Who needs it?

d)   What form should it take?

e)   How well are information needs currently being met?

f)   What role should ICT play?

g)   How do we enable information to be shared?

h)   How do we organise it all?

a) Why is better and more integrated information needed?

Information contributes to more effective integration in a number of ways. You need solid information available whether you are providing advice to people, planning new, integrated services or running them day to day.

Patients, service users and their carers all need access to up-to-date, and high quality, advice and information on the full range of services that are available across all sectors and what different services will cost. They need to be able to find out about health and social self care and self-help groups.

You will need to bring together comprehensive information on individual people's needs so that you can plan and prioritise the services you are offering them. But you will also need a much wider base of information to plan and develop the integrated service. You will have to bring together a wide variety of data on topics such as cross-sector service delivery, population and finances, so that you can assess needs and resources, make decisions on matters like charging and commission new service developments. You will also want to keep up to date with best practice in integrated services and service networks.

Three national policy drivers support these local information requirements. They are set out in government strategy papers – *Information for Health*, *Information for Social Care* and *e-Government* (see boxes 7a, 7b and 7c) – which we will refer to throughout this chapter. Some common themes run through these policies:

- **increased public access to information, and a faster response**. Care Direct, NHS Direct and LA customer contact centres aim to provide information and advice by telephone and, increasingly, via the Internet. The e-government (electronic government) aim is to make public services and information as accessible as the best of private sector services. So the trend is towards providing services at all hours, and

---

7a. Information policy drivers: *Information for Health*

- Fast and convenient public access to information and care – use of on-line information services and telemedicine, including NHS Direct and the National Electronic Library for Health (NELH)
- Lifelong primary care electronic health records – cradle to the grave information on individuals including summary information from electronic patient records covering treatment in the community, hospitals and mental health services and from electronic social care records.
- Round the clock access to patient records and information on clinical best practice – available to all clinicians, via NHSnet (the NHS Information Highway) and the NELH.
- Effective use of NHS resources – by providing NHS planners and managers with the information they need to support clinical governance, deliver the NSFs, produce local health improvement plans and the National Framework for Performance Assessment.
- Standards – a unique, lifelong, NHS number for each patient, standardising clinical recording, agreeing standards for security and confidentiality of clinical information, and implementing NHS wide networking and standards to enable data to be shared.
- Local Implementation Strategies (LIS) – showing how the *Information for Health* vision will be implemented locally, including interfaces with social services and other agencies.

Source: *Information for Health: an information strategy for the modern NHS, 1998 – 2005*, NHS Executive, 1998

Delivering the NHS Plan: Next Steps

- NHS Direct – expand the service and extend it to cover all out of hours calls to GPs and low priority ambulance calls.
- Implementation targets – 2005 for the electronic booking of all appointments across the NHS and electronic patient records in all PCTs and trusts by 2008
- Public information on performance – timely, comparable information on practices and hospitals, updated regularly.

Source: *Delivering the NHS Plan: next steps on investment, next steps on reform*, Cm 5503, HMSO, April 2002

---

on all days of the week, but with a more human touch. The extension of NHS Direct to cover out-of-hours calls to GPs and low priority calls to ambulance services are two examples. These services also provide people with a 'gateway' into services. This can include the direct booking of simple services such as 'blue badges' and, by 2004, will include the booking of NHS appointments.

- **joined-up services**. The integrated delivery of a service begins with an integrated response to people's first contact. The creation and linking of the electronic health and social care records will provide the necessary information base. The policies also require joint local information strategies between health and social care to be produced, as well as integrated e-government strategies across each LA. At a national level, the government is working on standards to ensure secure, compatible information systems that also respect individuals' rights to confidentiality and privacy.

- **improved service quality and effectiveness**. It is essential to keep abreast of developments in health and social care and integrated services and systems, as well as keeping up to date about what works well. The electronic libraries in health and social care will be important supports. Equally important will be the ability to make best use of local information in quality assurance and performance management. This is a major thrust in both *Information for Health* and *Information for Social Care*.

Although the information requirements of integration are vast, the majority of the information is already available. However it may be difficult to find, can be of variable quality and is often not being used in the structured way required to support effective evidence-based planning, management and service delivery. One of the early tasks you should be undertaking, therefore, is to put together a picture of what information is currently available and to whom, along with its quality and current use.

7b. Information policy drivers: *Information for Social Care*

- Electronic social care records – by October 2004, comprehensive, individual records, shared with service users, supplying social care information to the electronic health record, to Caldicott and BS7799 standards.
- Improving the quality of service through information management – each SSD: designates a senior manager as information and ICT lead; develops an information strategy, linked or part of, the LIS and or the LA's 'implementing e-government statement'.
- Information sharing – DoH to develop and promulgate protocols and standards consistent with *Information for Health* and liaise with the NHS Information Authority, the Data Protection Authority and others on data protection and sharing.
- Connecting with health – DoH to set dates and resolve issues of connectivity with health including, the use of the NHS Number, NHSnet and the National Strategic Tracing Service.
- Local government – participating in joined up LA wide, e-government electronic service delivery developments such as customer contact centres, smart cards, and web based access linked with Care Direct and NHS Direct.

Source: *Information for Social Care*, DoH, 2001

---

b) What information is needed?

Six main types of information are needed. They are:

- **information about the service system** – who does what and where, access details, eligibility criteria, charging policies and protocols for integrated working
- **individual service user details** – basic information, needs assessments, past service history and the current 'package' of services being provided, name of the key worker, and day-to-day logging of actions
- **service unit data** – costs and volumes of the services provided, staff workloads, and quality indicators such as waiting times and completion times of reviews
- **planning and resources** – how effective and efficient the service is in meeting people's needs, the consolidation of capital and revenue accounts, the application of funds, staff recruitment, training, job history, sickness, turnover and retirements.
- **what works** – local evaluations and access to national research, good practice, policy and inspection reports.
- **organisational processes** – staff roles and contact details, how major organisational processes work, tracking planning and decision making.

7c. Information policy drivers: e-government

- Economic competitiveness – enabling people to find work and develop new skills. Developing ICT firms and e-based enterprises such as dot coms and new media. Helping traditional businesses to move into the electronic age and providing the necessary ICT infrastructure.
- Ensuring public services are tailored to people's needs and preferences – 'e-enabled' services that are efficient, joined up and customer-focused (for example based around important experiences in people's lives, such as having a baby). Services to be provided 24 hours per day, 7 days per week, by public, private and not-for-profit partnerships, and making use of customer contact centres, one-stop shops, the Internet, telephones, PCs, digital TV, etc..
- Increasing democratic participation by making more extended use electronic vehicles such as electronic voter registration; electronic voting; citizens panels; on line debates with elected members; webcasts of cabinet and council meetings; the on-line tracking of policy developments; and so on.
- Tackling social exclusion and supporting civil society – setting up 'UK Online' centres in socially excluded communities; supporting communities of interest (e.g. webcasts from Mecca) communities of place (e.g. via local intranets and local history projects) and providing electronic support to voluntary organisations (e.g. a website for contacts and new ideas).
- Boosting public service efficiency – improved co-ordination through streamlined processes (e.g. electronic document management); improved communication (e.g. webcasts of workshops, publishing via the Internet and on-demand printing); flexible working (e.g. teleworking) and easier means of obtaining goods and services (e.g.electronic market places)
- Targets and strategies – best value indicator 157, setting the target for the electronic delivery of services. Implementing Electronic Government (IeG) strategies, covering whole LAs showing how they will meet the best value indicator 157.

Sources: e-government, ODPM, www.local-regions.odpm.gov.uk/egovt/index.htm

Most discussions about information and integration concentrate on 'individual service user details'. This information is central to service delivery; and it also raises important issues about how to assess needs and about the privacy, confidentiality and security of data. However, as you can see from our list above, it is only one of the six types of information: the other five relate to how the service system and organisations work. This is not surprising: integration is only going to work if people understanding what is going on and are able to navigate the system effectively. Where customer contact centres have been established for social care, they are finding that this kind of information is in high demand. Unfortunately, they are often also finding that such information is either difficult to obtain, out of date, partial or not well linked, and requires a major effort to bring it up to scratch. Investing time and effort into ensuring such data is useable will benefit not only customer contact centre staff themselves but also front-line staff and patients, service users and carers.

c) Who needs the information?

As well as being needed by individual patients, service users and carers and the general public, this information will be of use to professionals, managers, elected members and board members who are located in a variety of national and local organisations: health or social care organisations, including the private and voluntary sectors; care trusts and partnership trusts; LAs, PCTs and SHAs; inspectorates and central government; and university and research bodies.

d) What form should the information take?

It will need to take a variety of forms. Verbal information will always be essential, for the many conversations between patients, service users and carers, with staff and across staff groups. Written notes are needed, of course, to keep track of what has happened and what needs to be done. Some of this will be structured information, supplied on the many forms in use, for example, for assessments.

The moves towards customer contact centres and integrated assessments will have a big impact on what information is collected and the form in which it will be stored and retrieved. People will want to be able to gain access to information in a number of ways, often now referred to as 'channels'. Face-to-face conversations will increasingly include the use of video phones and kiosks. We have already touched on conventional telephone use with LA customer contact centres, Care Direct and NHS Direct. And, although electronic means – PCs and digital TV, email, voicemail, databases, internet and intranets storing coded information, electronic document images of paper records, video and voice clips – are set to expand exponentially, paper-based systems will continue to be a basic way of organising and making information available.

Providing rapid access to information at all times will be impossible without integrated ICT support.

e) How well are information needs currently being met?

To grasp how well your organisation's current information needs are being met, you will need to ascertain exactly what information different people require. Some people will want integrated information on individuals, others will only need to have access to aggregate information and some will want both. Most people will require information about the service system and some will want to know how the organisations work. The

---

table 7.1: How well are service user information requirements being met?
Example: Access to a service

TYPE OF INFORMATION	LEVEL OF INTEGRATION		
	INDIVIDUAL SERVICE USER	SERVICE NETWORKS	WHOLE SYSTEM
Service system		*Strengths* • Good leaflets on how services work together *Weaknesses* • No one-stop-shop to find out who should be doing what on a care plan	
Individual service user details	*Strengths:* • Assessments and care plans are shared with service users *Weaknesses* • Users have no easy, direct access to their records		
Service unit data			
Planning and resources			
What works			
Organisational processes			

Service users need access to their assessments and care plans to ensure they are accurate and up to date, and the agreed services are appropriate. Service users seeing and signing initial assessments and care plans is now common practice. But service users being able to directly access them, at will and up date them is not.

Knowing how local services are meant to work together to deliver a care plan helps service users keep track of who should be doing what. Leaflets provide basic help. However there is no easy way in which service users can directly keep track of who has done and should be doing what next to deliver their care packages.

---

differences in these information needs come not so much from the roles people play, such as 'service user' or 'front-line staff member', but the activities they are involved in, at the levels of integration with which they are concerned. In table 7.1 we have set out a partial example that analyses how well service user information needs are being met in relationship to 'accessing a service'; while table 7.2 shows a similar analysis for 'planning and service development'.

table 7.2: How well are service user information requirements being met? Example: Planning and service development			
	LEVEL OF INTEGRATION		
TYPE OF INFORMATION Service system	INDIVIDUAL SERVICE USER	SERVICE NETWORKS	WHOLE SYSTEM
Individual service user details			
Service unit data			
Planning and resources			*Strengths* • Planning and management documents are available to users *Weaknesses* • These can be difficult for non-specialists to understand
What works			*Strengths* • Good local links through to national 'what works' websites *Weaknesses* • There is no readily accessible help to weigh the information
Organisational processes			*Strengths* • New policy development tracking system *Weaknesses* • The ability to introduce new ideas is limited

Service users involved in the planning and development of new services require access to a range of information on: planning and resources; what works; and organisational processes. This will include: overall strategies and plans; information on the quality of, say, local residential provision; and new developments. Such information is often available but may either be too basic or presented in a way that is too difficult for the non specialist to understand. Information is also of little use unless users have easy ways of responding to it and knowing their views are being taken into account.

Is information used effectively?

The lack of accurate information on front-line service delivery has been a barrier to developing an evidence-based approach to activities such as quality assurance, performance management, commissioning and planning. However, as *Information for Social Care* points out, the fact that high quality information will be available in the future will not, in itself, change this position. Rather, senior managers will have to make a conscious effort to use this information in a structured way, and build information use into the organisation's 'culture'. They can begin with information that already exists. But they also need to concentrate their efforts into developing new information systems that the people

---

TRY THIS

Evaluating information provision

- Identify the main groups of information users.
- Apply table 7.1 and/or table 7.2 to the information needs of each group as follows:
  - Identify which of the following activities are most important to the group: self care; accessing services; integrated service delivery; planning and service development; high quality services.
  - If necessary, break the main activities down into more detail.
  - Use the table to identify the levels of integration with which each group is most concerned and the types of information it most needs
  - In each case, describe the current strengths and weaknesses of current information provision.
- Decide your development priorities and incorporate then into the LIP and LIS.

---

who use the data – front-line service deliverers, support staff, patients, service users and carers – will find directly useful. The best way to do this is to involve these people from the start in designing the information systems.

We believe that this culture of information use has to be developed one step further if service integration is to work. Picture this situation. Staff in a multidisciplinary team hold a case conference on the needs of an individual service user. Each member of staff turns up with his or her own well-evidenced analysis of needs, and suggestions about what should be done. They each have their own perspective, reflecting the service area they come from. To produce a person-centred assessment and care plan, the case conference would be forced to 'unpack' these service-focused analyses and reassemble them into one coherent whole. This would be baffling for the service user and their carer as well as wasteful of time and frustrating for the team members, each of whom is doing their best for the service user. The alternative would be to develop an integrated approach to assessment and care planning. Making the connections between the different aspects of need would become part of the assessment process. The case conference would find developing an integrated case plan a far more straightforward process.

f) What role should ICT play?

ICT has a number of roles to play in enabling the sharing of information. It could help to improve the means of communication (email, voicemail, video and mobile phones). It could help to provide direct access to information (shared databases, the Internet and intranets) as well as mediated access to information (access to staff, often by phone, who themselves have direct access sources of information).

ICT can also enable you to provide different levels of access to different people, based on agreed protocols about sharing information. For example, *Information for Social Care* proposes three levels of access to detailed health and social care information on individuals: 1) 'signposting' (checking which services a patient or service user is using); 2) 'basic service data' (finding out where the service user is – e.g. in hospital – the care plan, the dates that their assessment is to be completed and specific services or treatments started; and 3) full access (to enable joint assessments and to supply staff with the full information they require to provide an effective service).

The range of actual and planned ICT developments is vast. The main challenge is how to co-ordinate and link them so as to support integration at a local level. Once again, drawing up a 'map' of current and potential developments to show how they will support information use at the different levels of integration will help you to see the connections. Table 7.3 (overleaf) illustrates what might emerge from such an analysis.

Linked electronic records

The national developments linking electronic social care records to electronic health records are of fundamental importance to local service integration. The basic requirements of these records are outlined in Information for Health and Information for Social Care but, as the systems on which they will be run will be commissioned locally, it will be up to local agencies to make linked records a reality. This should be reflected in local health improvement plans (HIMPs) and be picked up in more detail in the local implementation plan (LIP) and local implementation strategy (LIS). In social care, the fact that the provision of electronic social care record systems is dominated by two major providers may prove helpful to the work involved in linking these records.

LA customer contact centres have a key role to play in: handling calls for information; screening and signposting new referrals; and providing a wider integration of services beyond health and social care. This capacity is being enhanced by *Care Direct* (see box 7d). *NHS Direct* (see box 7d) provides a health screening, advice and referral service. Much of the information about services and how they work is needed by all these customer contact centres. The centres also require access to enough information on individuals to be able to refer people on to other services and provide those services with complete, up-to-date referral information. So contact centres also need access to what *Information for Social Care* (see box 7b) refers to as 'signposting' and 'basic service

table 7.3: How proposed developments and challenges can affect the integration of information (some examples)

| TYPE OF INFORMATION | LEVEL OF INTEGRATION | | |
	INDIVIDUAL SERVICE USER	SERVICE NETWORKS	WHOLE SYSTEM
Service system	*Developments* Care Direct and NHS Direct and LA customer contact centres *Challenges* Producing an integrated response giving different remits		
Individual service user details	*Developments* Electronic health and social care records *Challenges* Producing an integrated record, overcoming problems of security and confidentiality		
Service unit data			
Planning and resources			*Developments* Anonymously linking data on individuals across sectors *Challenge* Getting organisational agreement and ensuring security, confidentiality and legality
What works			
Organisational processes			

• Individual service user: The main ICT developments are customer contact centres, Care Direct and NHS Direct and electronic health and social care records. The challenge is to make effective working links between these complementary developments that, in the example, are currently running in parallel.

• the whole system: Good information on plans and service developments is now available. However anyone not well versed in the language and concepts used finds the information difficult to interpret. This is a problem both for staff, working across sectors, patients, service users and carers and the public. The new system that enables policies to be tracked as they develop is good at providing information but not yet designed to enable people to feed in their own ideas in response.

data'. LAs are seeing to this by providing contact centre staff with selective access to the ICT-based systems on which personal and service history information is stored. It makes sense for health and social care integration to take full advantage of this developing infrastructure and make it an integral part of their information and ICT strategy.

Shared infrastructure

High speed networks are essential to handle the volumes and types of information that will be required to support integrated working. Without them, access to information will take too long. Staff will become frustrated and will either revert to existing paper systems or update the electronic systems only infrequently. Either way would be counterproductive.

This means that access to the high-performance NHSnet will be essential, as will a serious investment in and connection to high speed LA corporate networks. This also means that all agencies must develop the ability to comply with the security requirements for safeguarding confidential information, for example, those laid down in the NHSnet *Code of Connection*.

The growing use of smart card

7d. Care Direct and NHS Direct

Care Direct

- Advised people over 60 (could be extended to other age groups) on health, housing, social care and social security benefits
- Initially piloted in six LAs, it covered the whole of the south west by October 2002
- Free phone telephone, face-to-face help desks and website
- Aims to provide information and advice that people need, when they need it and, if they need support, have it delivered in an integrated way
- Delivered through partnerships between LAs and the DoH
- The service is sometimes linked in with an LA call centre enabling easy access to care management and one the spot booking of simple services. Many schemes have volunteers to befriend and help with tasks such as form filling

Source: www.doh.gov.uk/caredirect/index.htm

NHS Direct

- Covers: health worries; general health advice; information on local health services and on self help and support groups
- Nationally available 24 hour help line and interactive website
- Aims to reduce unnecessary visits to GPs by people with non life threatening or serious conditions
- Call handlers take basic information, nurses then use a clinical assessment computer system to check symptoms and advise on treatment
- Extensions to the core service include: monitoring and supporting people with chronic health conditions; ensuring people needing an ambulance service get it in good time
- Spin offs: accident and emergency department using a face to face version of assessment software to reduce waiting times

Source: www.nhsdirect.nhs.uk

---

technology and videophone kiosks in LAs will be of interest to health. Both of these technologies will offer great economies if they are put into widescale use. Agreeing ahead of time that some shared infrastructure is likely, identifying the possibilities and sorting out the principles of financing and managing it will pay dividends in speeding things up and avoiding potentially costly duplication. The development of secure and effective connections will also be helped by the introduction of national standards for LAs.[1]

g) How do we enable information to be shared?

Most of the barriers to sharing information arise in the use of personal

TRY THIS

Integrating IeG, LIP and LIS developments

- List the key developments within the LA's IeG statement and those in the LIP and LIS that have a bearing on integration
- Assume the developments have been implemented and use table 7.2 to identify any further challenges that you may need to address for them to support integration fully.
- Use your conclusions when you are designing and implementing the planned developments.

information. However precautions also have to be taken when information is used in planning and research.

Patients, service users and carers constantly complain about having to repeat the same information to staff from different services and of being used as 'human switchboards' to ensure staff know who is doing what. Staff, too, express their frustration at not being able to communicate easily. These are compelling enough reasons why information sharing should be accelerated. But getting agreement on what data to share, with whom, and how to share it can take time. There may be a number of barriers to overcome, privacy being one of the most important.

People have rights under Article 8 of the Human Rights Act (HRA) (see box 7e) to have their privacy respected: in other words, to be able to decide when to provide information on their private lives and to whom. Domestic UK law does not provide a definition of 'privacy.' Instead, the UK has relied on a common law duty of confidentiality. Nor does the HRA provide an unqualified right to privacy: it recognises that a balance must be struck between the rights of the individual and the interests of society. Many of the grounds on which public bodies can cut across the individual's right to privacy are covered by the statutes within which those bodies work. The Data Protection Act (DPA) (see box 7e) takes the HRA into account. Checking that information processing is being done legally and conforms with the DPA requirements and the guidelines of the Data Protection Agency should be a fundamental first step.

The introduction of the new NHS Number is an example of where the rights of privacy can be superseded. The mobility of people around the country, the different geographical areas and populations served by health organisations and LAs make keeping track of even basic information on patients and service users difficult. The health service is introducing a unique identifier, the NHS number, for all patients.

1. *e-gov @ local: Towards a National Strategy for Local e-Government*, ODPM, 2002)

Without this, it would be impossible for the NHS to provide a timely and safe service to mobile individuals.

The NHS number will certainly make a difference to health information systems and support integration, but will also have to link to LAs' systems. Social care records can include the NHS identifier, allowing records to be linked over the period when someone is using both health and social care services. But however it may be achieved, the use of a common identifier across health and social care is not just a technical issue but also a matter of public concern. Some people see it as an immense help; others view it as a way of breaching individual privacy. So it is essential to have a clearly developed rationale for its use and well thought through protocols to follow.

It is possible to overcome the barriers that privacy, security and confidentiality present to data sharing (see box 7f) . However, unless different groups of staff trust one another to collect the right information on their behalf and record it in a form they find useable, they will not act on it and the benefits of data sharing will be lost.

The Freedom of Information Act, 2000 (see box 7e) provides people with qualified rights of access to the personal information that is being held on them. This is essential if people are to feel confident that this information is accurate and up-to-date and that they have a proper say in their care plans.

People also have the right to assume that their personal information is being treated confidentially. This means using it only for

7e. Privacy, access and confidentiality legislation

Human Rights Act, 1998
- Incorporates the European Convention on Human Rights into UK law
- Article 8.1 of the HRA provides that 'everyone has a right to respect of his private and family life, his home and his correspondence'
- Public bodies may lawfully override this right where:
- Statutes require them to intervene
- There is no other less intrusive way to do so
- The following grounds apply:
- National security
- Public safety
- Protection of the economy
- Prevention of crime or disorder
- The protection of health or morals
- The protection of the rights and freedoms of others

Data Protection Act, 1998
- Covers the whole of the UK, replaces, and extends, the previous data protection act
- Regulates the collection, holding, use, disclosure and destruction of personal data
- The uses to which information is to be put must be lawful and registered with the Data Protection Agency.

Freedom of Information Act, 2000
- Right of data subjects to know whether their personal data is being processed, how it can be used and potentially be provided with a copy of the data.
- Right to have incorrect data corrected
- Right to prevent the use of data in direct marketing and a qualified right if its collection and use might cause unwarranted damage or distress.

In Scotland the Freedom of Information (Scotland) Act 2002, applies.

7f. Overcoming the barriers to information sharing

Caldicott Guardians

In the NHS, named after the author of the Caldicott Report, 1997, senior health professionals with responsibility for promoting clinical governance in their organisations are also responsible for:
- Updating internal protocols governing patients personal data including sharing with other agencies
- Developing policy on security and confidentiality
- Enforcing the 'need to know' principle
- Resolving local issues when they arise
- Improving the effectiveness of data base design, staff training and compliance

Social care departments have been expected from April 1, 2002, to appoint their own Caldicott Guardians (see Implementing the Caldicott Standard into Social Care, HSC 2002/003: LAC (2002)2, DoH, January 31, 2002).

Leeds General Protocol for Sharing Information Between Agencies in Leeds
- Provides an overarching framework covering all aspects of :confidentiality, privacy and security
- Makes detailed reference to all legal requirements
- Enables more specific protocols to be developed within the overall framework

Source: www.doh.gov.uk/ipu/confiden/guard/general.pdf

Information for Social Care Demonstrator Projects
Funded by the DoH projects relating to information sharing include:
- Integrated records – direct completion of a common assessment questionnaire on portable devices; integrated records supporting a single assessment process in multi agency teams; some developments focused on specific service users such as people with mental health problems and older people (Cambridgeshire, Kensington and Chelsea, Kingston, Leeds, North East Lincolnshire, Thameside)
- Security – generic tool for identifying and managing security of social care records; security and authentication options for linking to NHSnet (Newham, Suffolk)
- Public information – integrated health and social care website (Hillingdon)

Source: www.doh.gov.uk/scg/infsoc/ifsc/demonstrator.htm

West Surrey Electronic and Social Care Record Project

Covers primary and secondary health care and social care within adult mental health and older people's services. Record is accessible to accident and emergency, NHS Direct, ambulance service, social services emergency duty team and other out of hours services. Its key principles are:
- Access is on a 'need to know' basis
- Obtaining informed consent from service users
- The organisations are custodians of information owned by the service users

Source: 'Privacy and Data Sharing: the way froward for public services', Performance and Information Unit, Cabinet Office, April, 2002

the registered purpose and providing others with only the pieces of information that they actually need to know. Obtaining consent to share information should be standard practice. Where information is stored electronically, its proposed uses should be logged with the Data Protection Agency. As long as these uses are legitimate, and practice is in line with them, the DPA is not a barrier to information sharing.

In some cases, where trust exists between staff and where agreements about handling privacy have been agreed, the main stumbling block is that of security. Some health professionals are very concerned that, try as they may, LAs have not been able to make their systems as secure as those of the NHS. (In particular, they worry that other departments in the LA could get access to social care records.) Linking the LA into NHS data would potentially breach the security of the NHS system. However a number of LAs have developed secure arrangements that meet the NHSnet Code of Connection.

Information for Health and *Information for Social Care* have promoted attempts to provide a general framework on privacy, access, confidentiality and security. Meanwhile progress is also being made locally (see box 7f). Caldicott Guardians (box 7f) have an important role to play in developing effective information sharing practice.

Planning and research

A basic step in planning and research into how effective a service is, is understanding who, with which needs, receives what services, from which service providers, and with what outcomes. This requires data on individual patients, service users and carers to be joined up across health and social care and then stored for aggregate analysis (see box 7g). Because, for aggregate analysis, researchers and planners have no need to be able to identify individuals, the data can be anonymised by replacing names and addresses with a unique identifier.

However, while this may be intended to ensure security and confidentiality, in fact it often leaves enough information, such as date of birth, postcode and family details, for an individual to be identified. So it is important to ensure that further safeguards are in place. This generally means setting up standard protocols for handling such data. If these can be aligned across sectors, the integration of aggregate data is made easier.

> ## 7g. Integrating personal information for use in planning and research
>
> 'The Unique Pupil Number (UPN), allocated to all pupils, facilitates the linking of records by DfES statisticians. The UPN uses privacy enhancing technologies to ensure that the child's data are not misused but used for research purposes only. Local reference numbers are allocated by schools, which are reported, together with records of academic achievement and other core information, to the Department. At this stage the local number is translated into a different, national number which is used to create the longitudinal record.'
>
> Source: 'Privacy and Data Sharing: the way froward for public services', Performance and Information Unit, Cabinet Office, April, 2002

h) Organising it all

If you have made a commitment to service integration, it will no longer make sense to separate the information and ICT strategies of health and social care. Both *Information for Health* and *Information for Social Care* explicitly acknowledge this (see box 7h).

Integrated ICT provision

A multiplicity of systems exist in health and social care. In many health communities ICT services are shared, with one organisation providing ICT and other support services on behalf of others. NHSnet and NHS Direct, meanwhile, are provided nationally, and GPs invest in their own systems. In LAs, corporate systems provide shared services, supporting customer care centres and providing communications infrastructure as well as the main financial systems for each department. Any moves to use pooled budgets in integrated teams will therefore need to link through to these corporate systems.

If you are thinking of moving towards integrated ICT provision you will need to consider whether, or how far, social care should 'decouple' from such corporate systems and move into shared servicing with health, or whether the LA should become the provider of shared services. The latter may be more likely to occur where there has been large scale outsourcing of ICT and other support functions from LAs to external private sector

---

7h. Plans and strategies that support information sharing

Health: local implementation strategies (LIS)
- Local health communities agree collaborative investments in line with *Information for Health*
- LIS must support the HIMP
- LA, in particular social services, are core members of local health communities
- LIS management boards co-ordinate the work between local health communities.

Source: *Guidance on Implementing Information for Health: Number 2*, DoH, April 1999

Social care: local implementation plans (LIP)
- Produced by LAs summarising how they are implementing *Information for Social Care*
- Reports developments in multi agency working and information sharing
- Describes links with the LA-wide e-government programme

Source: *Information for Social Care: Local Information Planning, Guidance Notes*, DoH, June 2001

TRY THIS

Developing a local framework for privacy, access, confidentiality and security of information

- Download and use the Leeds framework (see Box 7f) to:
    - list the local information frameworks and protocols within, and between, the health and social care sectors
    - identify the main people and groups who need to be involved in developing a general framework and the forums through which this could happen.
- Gain people's agreement to develop the framework.

partners. Given the importance of the network infrastructures of LAs and NHSnet, it is likely that some shared resourcing will be a continuing feature of integration.

Organising for integrated information

The organisation of commissioning, provision and exploitation of ICT-based information systems is now beginning to receive the attention it needs within health and social care.

Organising for integrated information

- List the existing and potential information activities that are critical to the support of integrated services
- Identify who commissions and provides these activities and how they address integration
- Make any necessary changes to ensure the needs of integration are fully addressed.

Both the health and social care sectors are urgently addressing the need to upgrade and extend the range of their systems. The need to integrate information across sectors is also recognised, but is not as strong a focus for development. Given the pace at which service integration is now being driven, it is possible that new partnership organisations will find themselves using systems designed for a previous era. It is for this reason that we would argue that the continued development of ICT-based systems in both health and social care is not just to do with integration. Rather, all systems should be focused primarily on patients, service users and carers, not just on services and sectors.

But integration will demand changes in the way systems are planned and commissioned. Whilst there is cross-sector membership of both LIP and LIS development groups, the arrangements for translating plans into action still mostly lie within the individual sectors. Augmenting the joint planning within the LIP and LIS with an agreed approach to the integrated commissioning and use of ICT would help to focus people's attention on service integration. Integrated commissioning should, of course, cover information management and the use of non-electronic media as well as ICT. This would bring together activities as diverse as Caldicott Guardians (see box 7f), contracting with the voluntary sector, customer contact centres and the development of integrated ICT support.

Chapter eight: Governance

Governance is the set of activities that has to happen to ensure that organisations function effectively and are accountable to the people they serve or otherwise involve. There is no 'definitive list' of governance activities. But we find the following list, which we have adapted from the work of Adrienne Fresko,[1] makes a useful starting point. The functions of the board of governors in a public organisation include:

GOVERNANCE ACTIVITIES

1. Purpose and vision

2. Strategy and partnership

3. Delegation and implementation

4. Promoting excellence

5. Probity and accountability

1. Stating purpose ... This means stating the purpose of the organisation in a clear way so that everyone can understand it. For an integrated organisation, the purpose should make clear how individual users and carers will benefit from integration.

... and creating vision This will mean understanding what 'visions' of improved services people have, at a number of different levels, and translating these into a set of principles to guide the overall operation of the organisation. It includes activities such as translating national (government) vision – as expressed through policies – into a local plan that fits with the vision of improved outcomes that local people and partners have. This is one reason why involving users and carers is so important. The set of principles should guide your board's decision making and, again, involving users and carers will be an essential element of this, especially in seeing that principles are turned into practices that will lead to the improved outcomes.

2. Setting strategy ... This means setting the overall strategic direction of the organisation, in accordance with government policy and the needs of the local population. Good governance means putting patients', service users' and the public's needs at the centre of your strategic planning while ensuring that it is also in line with national policy and commands the active commitment of local partners. Pooling information and creating integrated information systems will greatly assist this process.

1. Adrienne Fresko, *Governance in the NHS, A discussion paper for the Board Leadership Programme,* London Region, NHS, February 2001

... **and developing partnerships** that serve the needs of local people. Good governance includes building and contributing to effective partnerships with local people and organisations to address inequalities in health and well-being. Again, this must include paying attention to the concerns of service users and carers in issue-based partnerships such as community safety, lifelong leaning and regeneration.

3. **Delegating and implementing.** Another role of governors is to agree policy and the allocation of financial, human and other resources to ensure the strategy is turned into appropriate action. They will need to clarify what decisions should be delegated to managers – and what they, the board, should retain – and provide the authority and resources to accompany that delegation. And accounting should be designed so that it is easy to trace the actions that follow any particular changes in budget allocation, discover who they are affecting and in what ways.

4. **Promoting excellence.** There are a number of ways that governors can promote excellence in an organisation. First, it is their responsibility to creating a 'climate' and 'culture' of service excellence and responsiveness, setting the tone for the whole organisation in the way it treats patients, service users, the public and staff. Second, they should be overseeing management and reviewing the organisation's performance. This involves monitoring and steering improvements in performance in line with national and local standards. It will mean accepting collective responsibility for achieving all national and local performance targets. Third, it is a governance task to promote quality in all aspects of the service. Best value, clinical governance and collaboration with external standards-setting and inspection agencies are all means of doing so, and your first step should be to develop an integrated approach to the national and local frameworks for quality assurance. Fourth, it is up to governors to safeguard the rights of the people who use the service or work in it. Considering recommendations that arise from complaints, listening to staff and 'whistle blowers' and promoting diversity and equal opportunities are all part of the governance role.

5. **Ensuring probity and accountability.** Governors need to ensure that high standards of financial probity and effective financial stewardship are upheld. This includes seeing that effective checks and balances and supervision are in place, co-operating with external auditors, and checking that the financial regimes will support the flexible and integrated use of resources. Finally, they are there to ensure accountability for the overall performance of the organisation – both to the government and to local people – and to enable effective scrutiny from outside.

What makes governance different in an integrated setting?

If you are only concerned with the strategic objectives of a single organisation, then the governance issues only apply to that organisation. But the strategic objectives that the government has set for health and social care involve many different organisations in

table 8.1: The implications of integration for governance			
GOVERNANCE ACTIVITIES	LEVEL OF INTEGRATION		
	INDIVIDUAL SERVICE USER	SERVICE NETWORKS	WHOLE SYSTEM
Purpose and vision	• Individual service users test how far the integrated purpose and vision are being translated into practice.	• Service networks are managed as integrated systems.	• Cross sector strategies are directly reflected in sector business plans.
Strategy and partnership	• Integrated information systems enable the quality and effectiveness of integration to be tracked at the level of the individual service user.	• Each organisation accepts collective responsibility for the quality and level of service received by individual service users.	• Implementing processes to co-ordinate market management activities with other organisations which draw services from the same markets and economies.
Delegation and implementation	• Services complement service user and carer skills and resources to co produce joint outcomes.	• The degree of delegation to local managers is harmonised across sectors to enable local network management.	• Strategic budget management covers the alignment and pooling of budgets as well as the knock-on effects of other changes to sector budgets.
Promoting excellence	• Aligning best value and clinical governance to focus jointly on outcomes for service users.	• Focusing on performance management of service networks as well as individual organisations.	• Strategic agreement on how to align the national performance and quality frameworks with local priorities.
Probity and accountability	• Ensuring effective processes for handling service user and carer complaints involving more than one organisation.	• External audits focus on the how the integration of service networks contributes to overall effectiveness.	• External scrutiny used to regularly examine the joint effectiveness, efficiency and probity of health and social care.

each sector and raise issues that cross the boundaries between sectors. They are concerned, too, with the wider factors affecting health and they treat patients, service users, carers and the public as active decision makers. This raises issues for governance at each of our three levels of integration, as we have illustrated in Table 8.1.

- At the level of the **individual service user**, service users and carers must be treated as equal partners, both in overall decision making and in delivering the service. The processes that the integrated organisation uses will need to be redesigned and integrated so that they are focused on service users and the outcomes they want to see achieved.

- At the level of **service networks**, it is the way local teams work together that provides the bedrock of integration. This cannot be left to chance. Governors should require, and support, the integrated management of service networks and insist that they accept collective responsibility for outcomes.

- At the level of the **whole system**, it makes sense to develop integrated commissioning and to integrate the management of services used by people with similar complex needs. It pays to remember, though, that all these people will also be users of mainstream services – such as primary care and customer contact centres – and so LAs and PCTs must ensure that the governance of specialist services is integrated with that of mainstream services.

Best value and clinical governance – the means by which LAs on the one hand and NHS organisations on the other try continuously to improve their performance – have a large number of common features. Both focus on outcomes for patients, service users and carers, but can often get diverted from this by the challenges of service and organisational change. LAs and health organisations will need to look for ways to align parts of the best value and clinical governance regimes into a joint programme focused on outcome for patients, service users and carers and service integration.

There are two major implications in what we have been saying:

- New integrated organisations will have to think broadly when deciding what sort of governance they need. For example, they will have to ensure that governance focuses on producing effective working links with mainstream services; they will need to be confident that their governance arrangements encourage everyone, whether their background is health or social care, to be working towards the same agreed outcomes.

- Existing organisations may need to change their governance arrangements to respond to the changes going on around them. For example, they are likely to want to adopt an approach centred on the wishes and needs of service users; and they may want to start judging effectiveness in terms of the joint outcomes that are being produced for service users as well as how well they provide their own service.

It can be easy to lose sight of

> ### TRY THIS
>
> Ensuring governance supports integrated service delivery
>
> Apply table 8.1 to the governance activities of your organisation:
> - Write into the appropriate cells of the table examples of governance that supports integration.
> - Identify gaps and decide which are the highest priority to fill.
> - Describe what needs to be done to fill the priority gaps.

outcomes when dealing with the intricacies of governance. If you want to avoid this, we cannot overemphasise the importance of involving patients, service users, carers and the general public in developing your organisation's 'vision' and ensuring it remains central to all you do. This vision should focus on tackling inequalities and social exclusion and producing more and better care than you do now. Pay attention to ensuring that everyone understands the vision in the same way and to tackling any historical accidents in the way resources have been allocated that may hinder you in achieving the vision.

The changing governance environment

Local governance is both complex and changing.

- **Adult social care.** In many authorities adult social care is being moved into one or more partnerships. The most common moves so far are to integrate mental health services and services for people with learning difficulties in separate provider care trusts or partnership trusts, often serving a cluster of LAs.

- **Primary care trusts (PCTs).** It is widely expected that many PCTs will merge. This may be more likely in unitary authority areas where there are two or more PCTs. Many of the mergers will be designed to overcome the diseconomies of scale of small PCTs. Others will be motivated by the desire to facilitate partnership working by aligning health services with those of the LA. Some PCTs are seeking to avoid mergers by proposing care trust developments with LAs, thus increasing the size of the PCT and overcoming the problem of diseconomies.

- **Older people's services.** The health and social care services that older people require span both mainstream services used by all the population and specialist services used mostly or wholly by older people. An example of the former is primary care and, of the latter, some forms of residential care. So we need to find forms of integration that can span both specialist and mainstream services in such a way that older people's needs can be met on a par with those of the rest of the population.

- **Children's services.** The transfer of adult social care services to partnership bodies is having an impact on the way LAs are thinking about children's services. Some LAs have already merged education and children's social care into single children's departments. Others may move in that direction either through choice or because, having changed their adult services, the remaining social care department is too small to be viable. This may be further accelerated by government proposals to allow the creation of children's trusts that could potentially integrate specialist services across education, health and social care.

- **Support services.** Any new care trust or partnership trust will require financial, ICT and HRM services to support their activities. The main choices are to be self sufficient or to share support services with one or more organisation. In the NHS, shared services – where one NHS trust provides finance, ICT and HRM services to a range of local NHS trusts – is being promoted nationally. In LAs, social care support services are typically split between departments and the corporate centre and, lately, there is likely to have been a large development in corporate ICT infrastructure to support developments such as call centres. If, in some smaller LAs, a significant proportion of support services, especially ICT, were moved into another organisation, this could reduce the viability of its corporate provision. But this would not be a problem where the LA had already 'outsourced' both the departmental and corporate support services to external private sector providers. Indeed, these providers are an alternative source to NHS shared services.

- **The acute sector.** In county council areas, and often in unitary authorities, the LA is served by more than one acute service provider located in more than one health economy. So integrated developments with the acute sector will require forms of governance that span these health economies. At the same time, some acute sector providers are moving away from simply providing services to becoming partners in developing the health of local communities. Alongside moves to prevent the need for acute sector care in the first place, or to enable it to be delivered in the community, we are also seeing examples of services being integrated between acute service providers to produce more integrated care for people. All of these examples of a changing relationship with the acute sector will affect the design of governance arrangements for new integrated services.

- **Strategic health authorities**. The role of the SHA will be critical in enabling system-wide integration, for example in the case where the LA population is served by more than one health economy. It also has an important role to play in ensuring that the concerns of patients and the public are acted on at the strategic level. The SHA is therefore an important part of local governance arrangements.

- **The independent sector**. The private and voluntary sectors provide a wide range of social care services and are playing an increasing part in providing health care. Health and social care commissioners commission residential and nursing home care from them and also have to manage the local market – including the supply of services from private and voluntary organisations – so that there is enough supply and enough choice. In some LA areas this is relatively straightforward as most of the care that is available is either purchased by local commissioners or directly by local people. But in other areas, where rising property prices and retirements of single owner operators have led to a drastic shrinking of the market, it is impossible to meet local demand from the local market. Other LAs, outside of these areas, then find that their local markets are being used by a range of neighbouring and more distant authorities, as well as self-funding service users. In these circumstances, discharging the governance duty of market management is complex.

- **Self-care**. Only a small proportion, on average, of any local population ever receives a service from SSDs. Older people, along with children, are the heaviest users of GP services but still only average four visits per year. So self-provided social and health care and directly purchased care (some of which is being funded through the increasing take up of attendance allowance) are important parts of the picture.

Self- purchased and directly purchased care are relevant to governance not only because of their impact on the demand for statutory commissioned care but also at a broader level of rights and responsibilities. To use an example – smoking and health care – there will be times when people's right to statutory care may be linked to their responsibility for self-care, and contested. Governance must be able to handle such debates when they arise. We think it's worth reminding oneself that governance does not just require the involvement of

> ### TRY THIS
>
> ## Will effective governance arrangements elsewhere fit your local environment?
>
> In their desire to avoid re-inventing the wheel, organisations will rightly look to other areas to check out effective ways of handling the governance of integrated services. To determine whether others' arrangements will fit your local environment:
>
> - Use our list under 'the changing governance environment' to make brief notes about the similarities and differences in the local environments of your own and other areas in whose governance you are interested.
> - Check whether any of the differences are significant in terms of governance.
> - Where differences exist, adapt the other areas' arrangements to fit your local environment.

service users but also of members of the general public, all of whom are self-carers.

Governance arrangements

Integration aims to improve services to people with a wide range of needs. For example, it covers services to older people and people with learning difficulties and those suffering from mental ill-health. Mainstream services used by children and adults and specialist services for adults will be targets for integration. The role of services such as housing, leisure, regeneration and transport that promote health and well-being must also be considered. It is unlikely that any single organisation could house all of these services effectively. More likely, integration will be achieved through a mixture of three linked types of organisations: single sector organisations; partnership organisations and arrangements covering whole system, markets and economies. And, if governance is going to enable integration, it must cover each of these organisational forms as well as the links between them.

a) Single sector organisations

Integration does not require all services to be relocated within joint organisations. But it does require each organisation to understand its role within the relevant service networks, markets and economies, and to contribute to agreed, collective outcomes. Single sector organisations such as acute, residential care and primary care providers will need to find a way to build this into their core business. And it needs to be reflected in their governance. Commissioning and contract management are two activities that have an important role in making this happen.

b) Partnership organisations

Used to pool or align their resources and activities within a single, combined health and social care organisation, a partnership organisation can comprise both commissioning and providing, or just one or the other. The organisation can offer services to the entire population or to specific groups of service users. The area covered could be an entire LA area, a subsection – for example, one or two PCT areas – or two or more LA areas. Table 8.2 lays out some of the choices.

In health and social care, partnership organisations are generally of two types: care trusts (see box 8a) and partnership trusts. A care trust, being an NHS body, is managed within the national NHS organisation. However the LA retains responsibility for the resources it commits to it, and for the health and social care outcomes for which it is responsible. Partnership trusts, on the other hand, are jointly owned health and social care organisations under single management but with a board that is jointly controlled by NHS and LA representatives.

table 8.2: Some examples of choices in forming partnership organisations					
	FUNCTIONS				
	COMMISSIONING ONLY		PROVIDING ONLY		BOTH COMMISSIONING AND PROVIDING	
POPULATION COVERAGE	Whole population	Specific user group	Whole population	Specific user group	Whole population	Specific user group
GEOGRAPHICAL COVERAGE Sub-area of an LA		*unlikely options due to diseconomies of scale*				• Care trust for older people's services in one part of Essex
A whole LA	• Brighton and Hove PCT and LA				• Barking & Dagenham combined PCT and social care department	
Two or more LAs				• Many mental health provider trusts		

There is a strong trend towards setting up partnership trusts rather than care trusts. The reasons for this trend are varied: some LAs object to what they perceive as having to hand over power to the NHS via a care trust; in other cases there is a positive wish to make the joint organisation a partnership of equals from the board downward; and some people appreciate the greater flexibility inherent in setting up partnership trusts outside of the DoH regulations for care trusts.

c) The whole system

The governance issues that arise at the level of the whole system can be complex, so it may be helpful to

> ## 8a. The organisation of care trusts
> - Care trusts are NHS bodies
> - Accountable to the SHA through the PCTs, and to the LA corporately, and scrutinised by the LA.
> - Two models:
>   — PCT: brings together both commissioning and providing, or just commissioning
>   — NHS trust: integrating provision only
> - Care trust board composition agreed by the partner PCTs and LA within the following constraints:
>   — Chairs appointed through the NHS Appointments Commission. Can be an LA elected member
>   — 15 members, including the chair,. Seven non-officer and seven officer members
>   — Non-officers will comprise a minimum of one LA elected member and NHS non executive members.
>   — Officer members must include the chief executive of the trust, the finance director, a senior social care manager, a senior nurse manager, GP or medical director.

take an example and look at it in detail. Consider an area that is governed as follows.

- Mental health and learning disability services are provided by care trusts, each covering three LA areas.
- All other specialist adult health and social care services are covered by an adult services partnership trust with a joint LA and PCT board.
- The area is served by two acute service providers, both located outside of the area in separate health economies.
- The adult services partnership trust purchases most of its residential care for older people from markets in the two neighbouring LAs.
- There is a significant amount of direct purchasing of social care services by service users and carers outside of the partnership arrangements and a large unmet demand for directly purchased domiciliary care.
- The LSP has a health focus within its social justice partnership which focuses on regeneration and tackling the broad issues of social exclusion.

In this example, many of the governance issues raised by integrating services will be handled effectively by the two new care trusts for mental health and learning disability services and the new adult services partnership trust. But there are other, broader governance issues that cannot be dealt with by these new trusts. They are: the governance of the health and social care system as a whole, including children's services; the management of the two residential care markets; and how to commission integrated acute services effectively from the two health economies.

There also have to be mechanisms for tackling other related issues. How can the overall balance of expenditure between the different partnership trusts be decided? Budget allocation requires a decision making process to be established between the LA corporately, wherever the directorship of social services is located, and the PCT. How can the LA scrutinise the whole system effectively? The LA must devise and implement an overall scrutiny strategy. And how do you ensure there is a consistent, integrated approach to tackling the factors affecting people's health? To comply with the duty of well-being, scrutiny of integration must be centred on people and the environment rather than focused directly on service integration.

In our example, the broader focus on health is developed through the health component of the social justice partnership within the LSP. This partnership co-ordinates all the work on social inclusion. However the PCT and the LA lead chief officer for social inclusion, and their respective cabinet members and non-executives, have the role of ensuring appropriate action across the LA and the NHS.

The LA has a responsibility to secure an appropriate development of the residential and domiciliary care markets that it and local residents use. This local market management is dealt with by the adult service partnership trust working with local providers, stimulating the local domiciliary care and respite care markets as well as taking on a liaison and joint market management role with the neighbouring LAs.

The PCT commissions acute services from two providers in the two separate health economies. In one economy the PCT is the lead commissioner on behalf of other PCTs; in the other economy another PCT takes the lead. However, in both cases, the local PCT is responsible for ensuring that the acute providers deliver services for its area and integrates them with the work of the local partnership trusts. The LA shares this responsibility for integration through its membership of the partnership trusts.

Designing a governance structure

Given the variety of different conditions and local objectives possible, it is unlikely that any one

---

TRY THIS

Evaluating the local set of governance arrangements

Check how well the sum total of your local governance arrangements meets the full range of integrated governance requirements.

- List the main groups of single and partnership organisations, care provider market and health economies management arenas involved in adult health and social care.
- Test the set of governance arrangements against the following.
  - Will integrated services commissioned by the statutory sector be well delivered?
  - Are self-purchased and directly purchased health and social care readily available?
  - Is the well-being of local people being safeguarded and promoted?
- Make appropriate adjustments to improve the local governance arrangements.

organisational form or overall set of organisational arrangements will suit all local circumstances. To decide on a suitable set of arrangements, you need to think about what will fit best with the processes of management and commissioning that support service integration aimed at achieving the outcomes users and carers want, while still ensuring appropriate accountability.

We cannot overemphasise the importance of form following function. Local governance arrangements should be able to deal appropriately and effectively with the three levels of governance we have outlined: a) single sector organisations b) partnership organisations and c) the whole system. However this does not mean that developing care or partnership trusts is necessarily your best next step. In some areas it might be preferable just to clarify and sharpen up the current practice. This might include clearly mandated and resourced joint commissioning or moving to lead commissioning and designated areas of integrated service provision. Whatever approach is taken, it must be part of an agreed plan about how, when and where to deliver better outcomes through improved integration. Otherwise, structures or new sets of organisational processes will be expected to produce results on their own. They won't.

LAs and PCTs are developing a variety of different governance structures. A few are moving towards the creation of care trusts, others are wanting to achieve integration through making full use of the health act flexibilities. The organisational environments include county and unitary LAs, areas with one or many PCTs and acute sector providers, places where integration is already well advanced and successful and places where it is still a struggle. While some are showing a preference for using care trusts and others just relying on Health Act flexibilities, this difference is generally considered to be minor compared to the need to find a robust and locally acceptable route to housing the new integrated arrangements. It is the aim of producing better outcomes for vulnerable people that must lie behind whatever local choice is made. But a variety of local factors have led different areas to adopt either similar or different organisational forms of integration. In the remainder of this chapter we will look at what the main factors are and what implications for governance they are likely to raise.

The existing system of service delivery

In making a move towards integration, some organisations are driven by a concern either to retain the current strengths or to tackle particular weaknesses in their existing services. For example, an LA may have strong and effective, locality-based social care management. But in the parallel health system, the links between the community nursing service and GP practices might be weak. As good locality-level integration is considered essential for effective service delivery, it would make sense to take the LA localities as the basis for integrating front-line services. These localities are already aligned with PCT and LA district council boundaries, which makes it more straightforward to develop flexible overall solutions to integrated commissioning and service integration. Similarly, some health economies are developing strong clinical networks. It is essential that, whatever means of integration is used, these should be strongly linked into the commissioning process.

Commissioning and planning expertise

Social care commissioning involves purchasing from a much wider range of organisations than commissioning in PCTs does. In social care, too, commissioning has typically involved a much more detailed approach to contracting and contract management than in health. This is why questions are sometimes posed about how to boost the commissioning expertise within PCTs, and what implications this raises for the role that current SSD assistant directors should play in the new integrated structures. In some areas, local politicians have given their support to integration mainly because of being assured that the SSD commissioning teams will be transferred wholesale into key positions in the new integrated structure. They see this as ensuring the continuity of 'a safe pair of hands' and as 'putting our people in place' in what would otherwise be perceived as an organisational arrangement dominated by health staff.

Further questions have been raised about the capacity of the new integrated structures to take part in planning and strategy development not just in health and social care but in linked areas such as community safety and influencing the work of the LSP. Because partnerships are an important route to gaining new national funding, the LSP will need to have access to a well co-ordinated planning function. This might well be housed corporately in the LA. Wherever is is located, any integrated organisation must have ready access to such planning facilities.

Workloads and the resources to support governance

As we have seen, integration can lead to complex governance arrangements. Will these improve or undermine the effectiveness of integration? In many areas, the resources available are already stretched and supporting this wider range of governance arrangements might be difficult. Each partnership will require senior managers and elected and non-executive members to devote some of their time, and there may not be enough time to go around to do the job properly. Finding enough non-executives and elected members with the willingness and the ability to work effectively at a strategic level is also a problem.

Both the NHS and LAs are concerned to limit the amount of money spent on management: if people are not sure whether the NHS restrictions on the amount of a budget that can be spent on management will also apply to the social care part of a pooled budget, their concerns are likely to be heightened. This might lead some organisations to work through partnership arrangements and partnership trusts, rather than care trusts, in the hope of avoiding some of the budget restrictions.

PCT development

A few LA areas share the same geographical boundaries as one PCT; others link to four or more. PCTs are themselves in transition and many are still getting to grips with how to develop effective ways of working within health. Many also face the possibility of a merger with other PCTs in the near future. Keeping as stable a base as possible from which to operate may therefore be a priority. So any wholesale movement into a partnership or a care trust might be unwelcome. This is even more likely where there are new unitary authorities who have yet fully to find their feet and are also looking for a period of relatively structural stability.

However, some PCTs – particularly if they share the same boundaries as the LA – would see the idea of moving into partnership or care trusts as less problematic, or even as an advantageous natural progression. Some will perceive that the organisational changes required are no greater than those of moving to PCT status and will want to push on. Others will adopt the middle position: to move forward with the use of Health Act flexibilities and reserve judgement on whether to make a further move into partnership or care trusts once the new arrangements are up and running and the degree of extra added value is apparent.

The role of GPs

The role played by local GPs is likely to be an important element in determining a PCT's stance on integration. In some inner city areas where there are many single-handed practices, GPs may have little or no interest in commissioning. In these cases, it is the stance of the PCT executives and non-executives that count. In other inner city areas and elsewhere, either large numbers of GPs or local leaders are very strongly committed to gaining control over commissioning and will therefore have strong preferences about whether and how the PCT engages in integrated working. In LA areas where there are several PCTs, it is possible to find that some PCTs are greatly influenced by their GPs and others are not.

Although some GPs may be strongly committed to PCT control over commissioning, this does not necessarily mean they will take the same position about integration. Some will be concerned only with health service commissioning, and see social care as a separate issue: these GPs are more likely to favour keeping a separate PCT. Others may see care trusts as a way of getting their hands on social care resources, which they envisage will be based in, or around, GP practices. Others still may think that PCTs are an unnecessary part of health service bureaucracy but may view care or partnership trusts as having a real effect on local services.

The LA's political and corporate stance

LAs differ in terms of which of the political parties, if any, is in overall control. Sometimes this can be very significant in determining their stance towards integration.

A few non-Labour-controlled LAs, and Labour LAs who are not on board with the government's full modernisation agenda, will not adopt care trusts as a matter of political principle. In other LAs, the politicians are taking a strong lead, often linked to their desire to drive forward the government's modernising agenda of joined-up working, community leadership, local strategic partnerships, modernised democratic arrangements, democratising the health service and tackling social exclusion.

In some LAs where politicians are not very proactive, it is the chief officers who have adopted and pushed forward this modernisation agenda. Other politicians may take a pragmatic view (or have no well formulated political view) about health and social care integration and the form it might take. In these authorities it is the views of chief officers and the corporate environment that will shape the LA's stance. There are also some authorities where neither the politicians or the chief officers have adopted a corporate stance towards the modernising agenda.

In LAs where the modernisation agenda is strong, it is easier to take forward discussions about health and social care integration. But the form that integration should take cannot be divined from the LA's corporate stance. Here, past experience of integration and differing views about the control of social and health care come into play. Where integration is strong, there may be a preference for building on the existing forms of organisation to take it further. This will be reinforced if elected members hold that the only legitimate form of governance is through open elections: they will want to go for making full use of Health Act flexibilities through partnership-style arrangements. On the other hand, where care trusts are seen as enabling the LA to democratise health and take forward its joint responsibility for the health of the local population, care trusts may become the preferred route.

Where integration is currently weak, people may favour care trusts or partnership trusts as a means to 'pick up the area by its boot straps'; or they may see Health Act flexibilities as providing a more gradual route through which to develop trust and experience.

The acute sector

The configuration of the acute sector provides a number of challenges to PCTs and to health and social care integration. The merger of acute sector providers means that any one provider will be serving even more PCTs than before. The difficulties lie in ensuring that acute sector providers who service significant national – and international – demand can also maintain an appropriate local focus, and in keeping an integrated local focus where an LA area is served by many acute sector providers. Part of the problem will be dealt with by pursuing new developments in primary care But acute sector provision can have a dramatic effect on social care, and vice versa, so it is essential to keep social care at the centre of this picture.

All of the acute sector developments confirm the need for PCTs to work together across the health economies that service their areas. when commissioning from acute sector providers. The developments also put pressure on PCTs to merge into larger groupings, thereby simplifying the co-ordination problem. Whether care or partnership trusts or other partnership arrangements are preferred, they will still have to be augmented by other governance arrangements to handle these sorts of complex negotiations.

The impact on other LA services: services for children

Most of the moves towards greater integration are focused on adult social care. Sometimes particular sectors are targeted – for example, mental health and learning disabilities – but, more often, this encompasses all adult services. If their commissioning and provision are moved into care or partnership trusts, this will have a significant impact on how children's social care services are managed as well as on the strategic social care role of the LA.

The removal of adult services will make it very difficult for social care to be sustained as a separate LA department. It is therefore likely it will be accompanied by some form of merger. The form it takes may be determined by existing developments. This can either be in response to the loss of revenue to the LEA through the devolution of budgets to schools or an LA-wide move, based on the modernisation agenda, to produce joined-up services for children. Not yet receiving much attention, but likely as a consequence of LA children's services integration, would be the integration of children's social care with health visiting and school nursing. Given the tripartite nature of the organisation, it may be that partnership rather than care trust arrangements will be preferred for children's services.

Governance and transparency

Decision making, monitoring and reporting arrangements need to be workable and transparent. The benefits of care and partnership trusts should come from having a single board to monitor and report on performance, with less likelihood of people attempting to transfer blame when problems arise. Governance options for the new integrated arrangements include a care trust board, a partnership trust board, or using an existing body if appropriate. It is likely that any governance structures will be used to control a large budget and

> **TRY THIS**
>
> ## Designing a workable governance structure
>
> The local factors, listed above, are critical to the success of any governance structure. Check your structure is fit for purpose by:
> - using the checklist of local factors to identify which have a bearing on your own situation
> - deciding how to handle the relevant local factors to ensure governance structures and processes best support integration
> - making any necessary changes to governance structures, and planning work on the priority governance processes needed to support integration.

wide range of services. The need for different professional groupings or services to be represented will have to be balanced against keeping board membership small enough to be effective.

It will be important, then, to ensure that the partnership boards have the formal and real power to enact their responsibilities and that participants have a common understanding of what it means to act as a board member and the responsibilities involved. This means being clear about when members of the partnership boards are individually responsible and when they are collectively responsible for decisions and actions. It will also means establishing clear and effective lines of accountability between the partnership board and its parent organisations. The governance arrangements will also have to handle the likely imbalance of power between health and social care that would arise from the greater size and complexity of the health economy. There is the potential, of course, for conflicts of interest to arise when the same elected members and non-executives sit on the boards of a number of local partnership organisations, all vying for a slice of the same overall LA and NHS resources. This is something to guard against.

Finally, you will want to ensure that whatever set of governance arrangements is decided on, it is kept as simple as is practically possible. Apart from anything else, an overly-complex set of arrangements will be difficult for patients, service users and the general public to understand, and will undermine their ability to play an effective role in governance.